"Jennifer may be blind, but she is leading people who are in the dark to really see God and to act on His empowering love."

"After reading *Lessons I Learned in the Dark,* I began to ask some soul-searching questions: Am I looking at those around me with my heart or with my eyes? What about my relationships with family and friends and my personal relationship with Jesus Christ? Jennifer challenges me with the statement, 'Unless we trade our fear for fight, we may never find the treasures that are hidden in the dark.' This book has prompted me to see God's treasures with a different set of eyes."

"Your story is a living witness to what God can do if given the chance! Your steadfast faith, Christian principles, and integrity will serve as a witness to many…my heart was touched!"

"Jennifer Rothschild allows us the privilege of learning the valuable lessons she's learned "in the dark" by shining light on her past and inviting us to follow in her footsteps. This journey is a page-turning, heart-shaping, eye-opening view into the life of a talented woman walking alongside the Light of the World."

D0092305

"Jennifer Rothschild is a vibrant reflection of the grace and faithfulness of God. I have been touched and challenged by her tender, surrendered heart and her powerful ministry."

NANCY LEIGH DEMOSS, SPEAKER, AUTHOR OF *LIES WOMEN BELIEVE* AND *THE TRUTH THAT SETS THEM FREE* AND HOST OF *REVIVE OUR HEARTS*, A DAILY RADIO MINISTRY FOR WOMEN

"With great depth, wisdom, and a light, joy-filled heart, Jennifer Rothschild shares treasures she learned in the dark so those of us who have the privilege of reading her book could continue our spiritual journey with more clarity, focus, and light. I highly recommend it!"

CHERI FULLER, SPEAKER AND AUTHOR OF *WHEN MOTHERS PRAY,* THE NEW RELEASE *WHEN TEENS PRAY,* AND FOUNDER OF FAMILIES PRAY USA

"What a treasure you hold in your hand, written from the heart of a godly woman. You will not only feel you are sitting in Jennifer's presence; you will certainly feel you are sitting in God's presence, learning to walk in faith."

ESTHER BURROUGHS, CONFERENCE SPEAKER AND AUTHOR OF *SPLASH THE LIVING WATER* AND *TREASURES OF A GRANDMOTHER'S HEART*

"For years audiences have been awed, inspired, and uplifted by Jennifer Rothschild's stories and songs. As I read this book and experienced again Jennifer's godly heart, I knew that God was truly directing her pen."

PEG CARMACK SHORT, EDITOR-IN-CHIEF, *BECOMING FAMILY* AND AUTHOR OF *A COUNTRY SAMPLER OF SIMPLE BLESSINGS*

Lessons I Learned in the Dark

Jennifer Rothschild

Multnomah Books

LESSONS I LEARNED IN THE DARK
published by Multnomah Books
A division of Random House, Inc.

© 2002 by Jennifer Rothschild

International Standard Book Number: 978-1-59052-047-5

Cover design by Koechel Peterson and Associates

Unless otherwise indicated, Scripture quotations are from:
The Holy Bible, New International Version © 1973, 1984 by International Bible
Society, used by permission of Zondervan Publishing House

Other Scripture quotations:
New American Standard Bible (NASB) © 1960, 1977 by the Lockman Foundation
The Holy Bible, New King James Version (NKJV) © 1984 by Thomas Nelson, Inc.
The Holy Bible, King James Version (KJV)
Holy Bible, New Living Translation (NLT) © 1996. Used by permission of
Tyndale House Publishers, Inc. All rights reserved.
The Holy Bible, New Century Version (NCV) © 1987, 1988, 1991
by Word Publishing. Used by permission.
New Revised Standard Version Bible (NRSV) © 1989 by the Division of Christian
Education of the National Council of the Churches of Christ
in the United States of America
Holy Bible, American Standard Version (ASV) © 1901 by Thomas Nelson & Sons

Multnomah is a trademark of Multnomah Books,
and is registered in the U.S. Patent and Trademark Office.
The colophon is a trademark of Multnomah Books.

Printed in the United States of America

For information:
MULTNOMAH BOOKS
12265 Oracle Boulevard, Suite 200
Colorado Springs, Colorado 80921

Library of Congress Cataloging-in-Publication Data

Rothschild, Jennifer.
    Lessons I learned in the dark / Jennifer Rothschild.
      p. cm.
Includes bibliographical references.
    ISBN 1-59052-047-5
    1. Rothschild, Jennifer. 2. Christian biography--United States. 3. Blind--United States--Biography.
I. Title.
    BR1725.R68 A3 2002
    270' .092--dc21   2002008167

07 08—10

I lovingly dedicate this book
to my first and greatest teachers, my parents,
Lawson and Judy Jolly.

Because of their faith, wisdom, and example,
I learned to see God.

TABLE *of* CONTENTS

With Heartfelt Thanks

To Judith St. Pierre, editor extraordinaire. Thank you for your skill and craftsmanship. I am most grateful for your love of God's Word and your effort to promote and protect the message of this book.

To Bill Jensen. Thank you for your guidance and enthusiasm. You've been both coach and cheerleader, and I will be forever grateful.

To Cheri Fuller, Karen True, and Peg Short. God used you in more ways than I can list to help me along the way. Thank you for your faithfulness to Him and for your friendship.

To Chris Hagen, my wonderful writing assistant. I am indebted to you for your tireless dedication and your extraordinary patience. May you never have to read this book out loud again!

To Phil, my husband. Who I am today is a reflection of your faithfulness to God and your unwavering commitment to me. I am honored to be your wife, and I will never outlive my love for you.

To Clayton and Connor, our precious boys. Of all the things in my life, you are what I'm proudest of and most thankful for.

To Beth Moore. Thank you for setting such a high standard for me. You have meant more to me than you will ever know.

To Don Jacobson and the entire Multnomah staff. Thank you for what you do for the kingdom. May God multiply your ministry.

To Jesus, my Lord and Savior. Your grace truly is sufficient for me. Thank You that, whatever my lot, You make it well with my soul.

Foreword

I remember the first time I saw Jennifer Rothschild. She was warming up on the keyboard in preparation for praise and worship preceding the message I had been asked to give at the event. I always look forward to meeting and interacting with the vocalist or worship leader where I speak because we are undoubtedly partners in ministry for that measure of time. I recall doing an immediate double take when I first saw Jennifer. I was oblivious to any challenges because I did not know her story and in no way could have guessed in a simple glance.

I have never tried to articulate what I found so unique about Jennifer until preparing to write this foreword. At the time I first saw Jennifer, I simply would have told you that something was wonderfully different about her. Now as I write in retrospect and with the aid of a few more years and a bit more experience, I can identify more clearly what I saw. She was so young, so fresh and beautiful, yet she had a knowing in her eyes that seemed unusual for one her age.

After I heard Jennifer's testimony, I had an "aha" moment and knew why her maturity exceeded her years. Not only did her eyes reveal a knowing; there was something indefinably *chosen* about her. From this vantage point I now know that I was seeing Jennifer not so differently from how

Jennifer sees most all the time—*with eyes of the Spirit*. I saw the invisible hand of God upon her. And I've never failed to see it since.

Years ago, when I was in my midtwenties, I attended a training seminar taught by Florence Littauer for prospective Christian speakers and communicators. I have laughed many times about receiving the seminar brochure in the mail because I wasn't on a mailing list and had little familiarity with Florence at that time. I'm convinced I received the application because I was pitiful and, in view of what God called me to do, He knew I needed emergency speaking assistance. I'm pretty sure He addressed the brochure Himself. I am definitely on *His* mailing list— even when I've tried to move. I learned a principle at the seminar that I still use as a plumb line for every message I prepare to speak or write. According to Florence each person must ask herself two critical questions before addressing any group:

"Do I have anything to say?"

"Does anyone need to hear it?"

Beloved, Jennifer Rothschild has something to say.

And all of us need to hear it.

Since the first time I saw Jennifer she has become a mother of two, a seasoned communicator, and a singer who can practically sing glory down on your head. Yet she still has that same freshness and graceful beauty that struck such a deep chord in my soul years ago. To my delight, Jennifer and her husband are also tremendous fun. I have an affinity for believers who don't view *godliness* and *good humor* as exclusive terms.

That's why I knew I was safe to make a spontaneous phone call to her home after seeing a photo spread of her and her family in a Christian magazine last year. The message I left on her voice mail went something like this, "Okay, young lady, I'm not about to leave it to your husband to tell you how you look in that layout. Men don't tell nearly enough details. Let me just tell you that you are stunning!" I then proceeded to tell her how sassy and cute her hair, makeup, and outfits were. It was strictly a girl moment, but I had a feeling she'd get a kick out of it. Then I read the article. And cried. Somehow Jennifer possesses that rare, God-given combination of lightness and depth. Grace and truth. Just like the One who called her.

Lessons I Learned in the Dark is gripping. I don't know the person to whom it has nothing to say. Jennifer Rothschild is the real thing. She knows what she's talking about. She does not have the luxury of telling and retelling a testimony from years past of challenges long since resolved. She lives in present tense, making daily choices to step over a plethora of seen and unseen obstacles. Jennifer is a living, breathing testimony still actively being written by the hand of God. I have a feeling this book won't be the last we hear from her. I am honored to recommend Jennifer Rothschild and her stirring new book to you. May God grant us all the gift of eyes that truly see.

Beth Moore

The
GREATEST
LESSON

Life is a fascinating school. Tucked in the corners of its dailiness are countless lessons, large and small. Some I've learned as a matter of course, almost unconsciously. Others have frustrated all my attempts to comprehend. I've raised my hand time and again in life's classroom, longing for answers. I've scrutinized the pages of its textbook, yearning to understand. I've walked its hallways and climbed its stairs, searching for its meaning.

We learn many of life's lessons when times are good and circumstances easy. Others, we learn only in seasons of hardship, loss, and great darkness. Although suffering can be the harshest of headmasters, its curriculum may open the door to freedom beyond our loftiest expectations. *Sometimes it's only in the adversity we dread that we begin to discover the kind of life we've only dreamed of.*

That was the lesson God began to teach me in 1979....

I began my sophomore year of high school experiencing all of the usual teenage changes.

But there had also been one very unusual one.

Near the end of junior high school, I began to realize that my eyesight was deteriorating.

As I picked my way carefully through the packed hallways of Glades Junior High, I was amazed at how my classmates streamed through the crowd with such ease—even in dark stairwells. How could they do that without bumping into schoolmates or lockers? When we played softball in P.E., I couldn't understand how my teammates could catch the ball so easily. I would stand out in right field, glove in hand, and stare intently at the ground, trying to see the shadow of the approaching ball. Then I'd listen to where it landed and hope I could find it.

My math grades were beginning to drop because, even though I didn't know it at the time, I couldn't see the difference between a 3 and an 8. My friends could see the numbers on the telephone pad, while I hadn't been able to see the numbers on my locker for months.

Difficult as it was to admit...I began to realize that it wasn't normal for me not to be able to see a softball in the air, the stairs in a stairwell, or the numbers written on a blackboard. As a result, I began to feel more awkward and self-conscious. At last I became so concerned that I told my mother, who (as you might imagine) immediately took me to an ophthalmologist.

The eye doctor tried to remedy my failing sight with prescriptions for stronger glasses, but they didn't help. Eventually, he referred me to an eye hospital.

After several days of testing, the doctors at the Bascom Palmer Eye Institute met with my folks and me in a conference room. They told us that I had retinitis pigmentosa, a degenerative disease that slowly eats away the retina of the eye.

There was no cure, and no way to correct damage already done.

The doctors said I had lost so much vision that, at fifteen, I was already legally blind. And they told us that my retinas would continue to deteriorate until I was totally blind.

Blind...totally blind.

The words sounded so final. So certain. So cold. I felt a chill inside that I'd never felt before. Maybe that's what finality feels like. It was almost surreal.

Nothing else was said. Silence fell upon that conference room like shadows fall just before night, and it shrouded us as we left the hospital, walked across the parking lot, got in the car, and journeyed home.

I have often thought that it was probably much harder for my parents that day than it was for me. Yes, my eyes were being robbed of sight, but their hearts were being crushed. Can you imagine their heartache? Can you hear the sound of that door slamming in their souls? Surely one of life's greatest sorrows must be to watch your child suffer…and to feel helpless to prevent it.

My dad gripped the steering wheel tightly as he piloted us home through the spidery Miami streets. I could only imagine the prayers he must have been praying. He had always been my source of wisdom, my counselor, my comforter, my rescuer, and the one man I trusted completely. And even though he had also been my pastor, not even more than twenty years of ministry could have prepared him for this moment. I wonder if he was thinking, *Dear Lord, how can I fix this?*

Yet on the ride home he was silent.

My mother sat next to him in the front seat. I could feel her broken heart. A mother's heart is so tender. I don't know any mother who wouldn't willingly trade her own comfort to ease the suffering of her child. I wonder what her prayers were like on that day. My mom was my standard, my cheerleader, my encourager, my mentor, and my friend. I think she must have been wondering, *Will she be safe?*

Yet on the ride home, she too was silent.

I had always been strong willed, trusting, sensitive, and talkative. Yet sitting in the backseat on the ride home that day, I also kept silent. I remember the reasons for my silence as if it were yesterday. My heart was swelling with emotion, and my mind was racing with questions and thoughts. *How will I finish high school? Will I ever go away to college? How will I know what I look like? Will I ever get a date or a boyfriend? Will I ever get married?* I remember feeling my fingertips and wondering how in the world people read Braille.

And then it hit me.

I would never be able to drive a car.

Like most teenagers, I thought that having wheels was just like having wings. I couldn't wait to drive! That was a step toward independence to which nothing else compared. But now it was a rite of passage I would never experience, and I was crushed.

After forty-five long minutes, we arrived home. Once inside, I went immediately to the living room and sat down at our piano. It was old and stately and had a warm, comforting sound. For me it was a place of refuge.

By then I had been playing the piano for several years. In fact, I'd had almost five years of lessons. The funny thing about my lessons, though, was that I'd managed to stretch them out over an eight-year period. I was one of those kids who would *beg* my mother to let me take piano lessons—and then after about six months *beg* her to let me quit! Three or four months later we'd start the whole routine over again.

I barely muddled through my lessons with many piano

teachers, and I'm sure it wasn't pleasant for the listener to hear me practice what I'd learned. Let's just say that I was a little short on natural talent! I did, however, practice diligently every night after dinner. That's because if I did, I was excused from clearing the table and washing the dishes.

But this time was different.

I wasn't seeking refuge from chores, and I didn't play just the few songs I'd memorized. Instead, I began to play by ear, and the melody that filled the living room that afternoon belonged to a song I'd never played before. My fingers followed a pattern along the keyboard that was new to me, yet...somehow familiar.

The song I played was "It Is Well with My Soul."

I think God guided my heart and hands to play that hymn. Some people have told me it was a miracle that I could sit down at the piano that day and begin to play by ear for the first time. Perhaps it was. Who knows? But to me, there was a bigger miracle that day, that dark day of shock, loss, and quiet sorrow.

The real miracle was not that I played "It Is Well with My Soul," but that it actually *was* well with my soul.

On that day more than twenty years ago—in the hospital, on the ride home, and at the piano—even as I mourned my loss, I looked into the heart of my Teacher. I knew His Word and His character, and they were what allowed me to say, "Whatever my lot...it is well with my soul."

Today I still sit at the piano and play by ear. I listen to books on tape. I walk with a cane and rely on others to drive me places. I know well the trappings of blindness. I understand the isolation and hardships it can bring. Yes, blindness can be painful—all life's heartaches are—but through it, God has taught me the greatest lesson to be learned in the school of suffering: *Even when it is not well with our circumstances, it can be well with our souls.*

That is the first and greatest lesson I learned in the dark, and the foundation for all the lessons that have followed.

When peace like a river attendeth my way
When sorrows like sea billows roll
Whatever my lot, Thou hast taught me to say
It is well, it is well with my soul

Not by Sight

Though my eyes may see darkness
    and the lamps be dimly lit
I can see beyond this earthly shell
For the faith that brought me so far
    gives me hope to carry on
For my eyes will behold Him someday

We walk by faith not by sight
Looking through His eyes
I can see the light
The Morning Star shines so bright
    until our faith becomes sight

Earthly dreams and shadowed pictures
Of the one I used to be
*   were left to become the one I am*
And though my mind may not understand
*   with my eyes I'll look to You*
For You are the substance of my faith

We walk by faith not by sight
Looking through His eyes
I can see the light
The Morning Star shines so bright
*   until our faith becomes sight*

One

TAKE *the* FIRST STEP

M y friend and I stood in the hallway of my new home exchanging decorating ideas. When I commented on how much I loved the wallpaper in my hall bath, there was an awkward pause.

"But Jennifer...how do you *know* you love the wallpaper if you can't see it?"

It was a fair question.

I told her that my mother had described the Jacobean print to me in vivid detail, and that with every word I heard, I fell more in love with it. In my mind's eye I could see the honey mustard, cranberry, and forest green colors twining through the vines and leaves on the wallpaper.

It's funny: Even though I couldn't see, I could see it.

That's how I like to explain faith sometimes. The dictionary says that faith is a firm belief in something for which there is no proof—a belief that does not have to rest on visible evidence. Just because my eyes can't see the design of the wallpaper doesn't mean it's not there. I *know* it's there, so my eyes don't have to confirm what I know is real. In fact, it's so real that even though I can't see it, I can still enjoy and delight in it.

I think that's what the writer of Hebrews had in mind when he wrote, "Faith is the substance of things hoped for, the evidence of things not seen" (Hebrews 11:1, NKJV). If we understand that this is what faith is, we can exercise it in the confidence the apostle Paul talked about when he said, "We walk by faith, not by sight" (2 Corinthians 5:7, NASB). Walking by faith is acting upon a reality not yet seen.

Relying on sight in our faith walk never allows us to accomplish God's best. What's more, it never reveals the hidden treasures that only the eyes of faith can see. But most of us never learn to walk by faith...until we learn to walk in the dark. We don't lean on God until fear makes us feel shaky and weak.

SHAKY STEPS

On a warm summer afternoon in 1982, my mother and I sat down on the soft grass under the silk oak tree in our front yard for our final heart-to-heart talk of the summer. It was August 14, and the next day I would leave my home in

Miami for Palm Beach Atlantic College.

In the three months since I'd graduated from high school, we'd spent every day preparing me to go. Mom and I had shopped for a new wardrobe for me and bought furnishings for my dorm room, including a much-coveted rainbow comforter.

During that long, lingering summer, I'd also spent several weeks in "mobility training"—that is, learning to walk with a cane. The Lighthouse for the Blind assigned me an instructor named Mike, who diligently taught me how to use my new cane so that I would be as self-sufficient as possible in my new setting. Mike taught me all the techniques I'd need to know as I learned to walk in the dark.

By mid-August the U-Haul was loaded, my suitcases were packed, and I knew how to walk with my cane. I was ready for college and rarin' to go. Then on August 14, my confident expectation suddenly turned to dread. The frightening reality of leaving home squelched all the excitement of preparing to be an independent college student.

I was leaving behind my sense of security.

I was leaving behind the comfort of familiar surroundings.

I was leaving behind all that was well-known and safe, trading it in for a new kind of darkness that was unfamiliar and scary. When I began to weigh the new clothes, the new dorm furnishings, and the new cane against the security of my old friends and my old room, my heart froze with fear.

As my mother and I leaned against the tree that afternoon, I suddenly cried, "I *can't* go to college, Mom! Who's going to check my makeup for me? Who's going to make sure my clothes aren't wrinkled or stained? Who's going to tell me what food is on my plate? How will I really know if there are no cars coming when I'm trying to cross the street?"

My tears soon drowned out my questions. "Please don't make me go, Mom," I begged.

My mother gently consoled me. Then she said, "You have to go to college, honey. We've prepared you to go, you've chosen to go, and deep down you want to go to college. But...," she continued, wiping away her own tears, "you only have to go for two weeks. If you really can't handle it, your dad and I will come get you. And you can even keep your new rainbow comforter!"

So when the sun rose on August 15, Dad got behind the wheel of the U-Haul, Mom and I loaded my suitcases and our heavy hearts into our Ford Fairmont, and we drove north to West Palm Beach. After we arrived and unloaded, we hugged good-bye, and they got back in the car and headed south.

Now I was alone with my fear, and suddenly I felt blinder than ever. It was the emptiest feeling I'd ever had. Walking in the dark was scary enough, but walking *alone* in the dark was terrifying.

But I believe that where there is fear, there is fight! My

terror fueled my tenacity, and for two weeks I held on doggedly. I was determined to make it until I could legitimately call home and say, "I'm sorry. I tried. It's not working. Please come get me!"

During that time, I used my cane to navigate the campus just the way Mike had taught me, and it helped me feel a little less scared. Then one day I tapped my cane into the cafeteria, and there I found an unexpected treasure.

It was a guy.

Not just any guy, mind you. This guy was the handsomest and most charming and intelligent guy I'd ever stumbled upon. His name was Philip Rothschild, and we quickly began to spend time together. Let's just say that I barely noticed when the two weeks had passed. But I did call my mom just to say, "Please don't ever make me come home from college!"

Here's the lesson I learned: *Unless we trade our fear for fight, we may never find the treasures that are hidden in the dark.*

I found my future husband when I chose to risk walking in the dark. It's the same with our spiritual walk. It's often scary. Most of the time, God doesn't reveal what's next—and we can't begin to anticipate what the future holds. But most of us never learn to walk by faith until we first walk in the dark.

As a loving Father, God says, "You must take a step. I've prepared you to go, and deep down you want to walk by faith." When we do step out, like the heroes of the faith in Hebrews 11, we'll find the treasures that God has reserved for those who lean completely on Him.

A STEADY PACE

I believe that one of the ways God wants us to learn to walk by faith is by following the examples set for us in the Bible. In fact, Paul writes, "Brethren, join in following my example, and observe those who walk according to the pattern you have in us " (Philippians 3:17, NASB). We need to observe those who walk well and follow in their footsteps.

All the amazing folks in the Hall of Faith in Hebrews 11 knew how to exercise "spiritual mobility"—they knew how to walk by faith, not by sight.

And all of them learned how by walking in the dark.

They didn't understand God's plan when they began to carry it out, and they didn't know what was coming next when they took that first step. Their faith became realized only as they *exercised* it—as they began to put one foot in front of the other. They chose to rely on something greater than what they could see or understand.

They chose to walk by faith.

And they can teach us how to walk with them on that path.

Noah teaches us how to go against common sense when we sense God in an uncommon way. Imagine if he had relied on sight rather than faith. Instead of building an ark, he might have opened a petting zoo!

Abraham teaches us how to willingly obey even when we don't understand. If he had been relying on sight as he trudged up Mount Moriah, he might have been scanning the bushes for a lamb instead of obeying God.

Sarah teaches us that it's possible to believe the impossible. Surely it was not "sight" that prompted her to knit tiny blue baby blankets at her age!

Moses teaches us how to value God's reward more than man's riches. If he had been walking by sight, he probably would have milked his position as Pharaoh's grandson for all its royal worth.

You get the idea. It was faith that prompted Noah, Abraham, Sarah, Moses, and the other heroes of Hebrews 11 to step out the way they did. Faith always propels us to action.

But walking by faith isn't always easy. I'm sure that each one of those Hebrews 11 heroes went through some wrenching internal agony along that walk of faith.

Noah experienced it, pounding one more nail into a ship in the middle of the desert. Sarah felt it with a baby's tiny kick in her once sterile womb. Abraham knew it when he lifted that gleaming blade heavenward, ready to plunge it into the chest of his beloved son. (Who can imagine the agony and terror of that moment?)

And let's not forget Moses. He felt so out of his league that he begged God to send his brother Aaron to plead with

Pharaoh. I can just hear him: "God, I stutter like M-M-Mel Tillis, but Aaron—he sings like M-M-Mel Tormé!" All of us feel the ground shaking beneath us when we step out in faith. But even if we feel insecure, walking by faith requires us to take a risk. To take a step.

A CONFIDENT STRIDE

When I was learning to walk in the dark, what made it easier to risk walking with a cane was knowing that Mike was right next to me. If I felt wobbly, I knew I could hold on to him. If I reached out or cried out, he was right there. On our walks, he would quickly extend his arm when I'd lose my footing or become disoriented.

In the same way, when we feel shaky in our faith walk, we can hold on to God. Leviticus 26:12 reminds us that God Himself walks among us because we are His people. His strong arm is always there to help us. We can reach out for Him in the dark, and He will be there every time. And just as Mike patiently listened to me when I told him my fears, God will patiently listen to ours.

Learning to walk by faith is very much like learning to walk in the dark. The mobility techniques Mike taught me gave me security in my stride, and they're the very ones we need to apply to walk by faith. Check out the following tips for spiritual mobility and ask God to show you if you need a little instruction from Him in your faith walk.

Remain centered

As I learned to maneuver with my cane, Mike stressed the importance of remaining centered. He showed me how to hold my cane in the center of my body. Then with a steady arm, I would move my wrist from left to right. I did this in order to walk in a straight line and stay oriented. It allowed me to tap the sidewalk with the tip of my cane just before my next step, helping me anticipate any changes in my path.

It's also essential to remain centered as we learn to walk by faith. Losing your center will lead you astray. "Let your eyes look directly ahead and let your gaze be fixed straight in front of you," Solomon advises. "Watch the path of your feet and all your ways will be established. Do not turn to the right nor to the left; turn your foot from evil" (Proverbs 4:25–27, NASB). Being centered keeps you on your intended path.

When we stay on God's path and allow Him to be the center of our lives, we won't get disoriented when life falls under a deep shadow. When every step is steady, we won't slip, even when the ground buckles beneath us. "My steps have held fast to your paths," says the psalmist. "My feet have not slipped"(Psalm 17:5, NASB).

What is the center of your life? Have you lost your orientation?

Follow a mental map

I also learned that it was essential to know exactly where I was going. No aimless strolling when you are blind! Mike told me to think through my path before I took the first step and to always have a map locked in my mind. Knowing where I was going made every step purposeful and prevented missteps and mishaps. The map for a Christian is God's Word, and when "the law of his God is in his heart[,] his steps do not slip" (Psalm 37:31, NASB).

When we know God's precepts, they guide us. "The steps of a good man are ordered by the LORD" (Psalm 37:23, NKJV). But they also protect us. Paul says that the sword of the Spirit is the Word of God, a part of the armor of light that protects us against the dark powers of the world (see Ephesians 6:12, 17 and Romans 13:12). This world is a dark and shadowed place at times. If we naively step out unprotected, we'll be susceptible to the evil influences of the darkness around us. But if we wisely follow the map God has given us in His Word (no aimless wandering!), it will guide and protect us, making each step of our walk intentional. Then we can say with Paul, "I run straight to the goal with purpose in every step" (1 Corinthians 9:26, NLT).

What guides your steps? Do you follow the Master's map?

Listen to the Teacher

As I learned to use my cane, I felt my senses awakening in a whole new dimension. I became aware of the smell of diesel fuel from the buses that roared down the main street of my neighborhood. And as Mike encouraged me to tune in to the music of the motor, I learned to hear the difference between the sound of an engine when a car was in full motion and when it was idling at a red light. Learning to recognize what was coming (and how fast) helped me know when it was safe to go—or when I'd better stop and wait.

To walk by faith, we need to tune in to the voice of our Teacher. Isaiah 53:6 reminds us that we are all like sheep who have gone astray. And like sheep, we need a shepherd. But in order to hear the voice of our Shepherd above the din of all the other voices in our lives, we must be tuned in. We must *learn* to recognize His still, small voice.

Jesus said, "My sheep listen to my voice; I know them, and they follow me" (John 10:27). His sheep hear and follow Him because they are familiar with His voice. When we learn to discern the Holy Spirit's voice, we'll know when to go and when to stop.

As the prophet Isaiah wrote:

Although the Lord gives you the bread of adversity and the water of affliction, your teachers will be hidden no more; with your own eyes you will see them. Whether you turn to the right or to the left, your ears will hear a voice behind you, saying, "This is the way; walk in it." (Isaiah 30:20–21)

Are you tuned in to the voice of the Master? Do you recognize His voice as it resonates through your soul?

Jesus said, "God is spirit, and his worshipers must worship in spirit and in truth" (John 4:24). Walking by faith means that we allow the Holy Spirit to illuminate our eyes so that we can see beyond the here and now. Eyes of faith see every problem as solvable because they see every problem as spiritual in nature. What is merely physical is confined by the laws of nature, but what is spiritual has no confines except those our supernatural, sovereign God chooses.

This means that as we walk by faith, the Holy Spirit will help us fix our eyes on the source of our help, not on the sting of our problems. He will whisper in our ears the gentle reminder that "now we see in a mirror dimly, but then face to face" (1 Corinthians 13:12, NASB). Someday the faith by which we walk will become sight, or as St. Augustine put it, the reward of our faith will be to *see what we believe*. Can you see how important it is to walk by faith? Look where it will eventually lead us—face to face with God Himself!

"I am the light of the world.
Whoever follows me will never walk in darkness,
but will have the light of life."

JOHN 8:12

Never Alone

Never alone
In my darkest hour I am never alone
Not far from home and I can feel You near me
For I am never alone

In the midst of trials there is a triumph that I know
While trusting in the One who never changes
And though my heart grows weary in the struggle of it all
I have such assurance that You hear me when I call

Never alone
In my darkest hour I am never alone
Not far from home and I can feel You near me
For I am never alone

WORDS AND MUSIC BY JENNIFER ROTHSCHILD © 1990 ROTHSCHILD MUSIC (ASCAP)

prayers :

Ruby - Equador trip
    moms appts. + wisdom on situation
    guidance on college for Brian

Kath - Julie
    this weekend

Kathy - Finances + learning curve
    + property situation   33rd
                                 Blue Fruitridge
    Nathan - job + salvation   Franklin

Karen - Jenny & son to get jobs.
    mom arriving Oct 25th
    No gossip

Donna - Pain - help free her & sick
    Husband situation
    Job situation, giving her
    Lynn - Kayln (fear of future)
    Alex - son in law + salvation
    Lynns fear of the future

Two

GIVE YOUR GUIDE *a* TASTE TEST

I've had many guides since the onset of blindness. In fact, there are very few places I can go without one. Over the years my guides have included an entire cast of characters. I've held on to the arms of strangers in airports and the hand of my ninety-five-year-old grandpa. I've had tall, staid men and short, squirmy boys guide me. A few women who've walked with me have said very confidently, "We're going left here," as they very conspicuously turned to the right. (Sorry, girls, but there are some among us who are directionally challenged!) In college, I had a guide named Karen and, more recently, one named Stephanie. Both these friends are in wheelchairs, so I hold the handles, they push go…and we're off! My guides walk or roll. I trust.

You know what qualifies someone to be my guide?

Sight!

Let's face it, though. Just because people can see better than I can doesn't mean they're worthy of my trust. Trust is a choice I make. Trust is a risk I take. Why? Because otherwise I'd never go anywhere! The journey is worth the risk.

The members of my family were my first guides. My brothers were in elementary and middle school at the time, and they learned the basic techniques right away. I would loosely grip the elbow of one of them and walk next to him. This meant, of course, that we had to touch. How painful for them! How agonizing for me! Cooties may be invisible, but believe me, they exist. We all had to swallow our pride.

We were taught that when we came to narrow halls or doorways, my guide was to gently pull his arm behind his back. That was the signal for me to get behind instead of beside. It worked well. My brothers learned to quickly count steps, bark commands like *left!* or *right!* (they loved that part), and describe our path using a clock: "Branches at two o'clock...*duck!*" They learned to guide, and I learned to trust them as my guides.

It was pretty easy to trust my family to guide me. We already had a relationship, so it didn't seem like much of a risk. I *knew* I could trust them. Nevertheless, I still had to *choose* to trust them.

The apostle Paul reminds us that our heavenly Father has grafted us into His family through our faith in Jesus Christ, and that Jesus Himself pursued relationship with us so we could come to know and trust Him (see Galatians 4:5–6 and 1 Peter 3:18).

Still, it's not always natural or easy to trust God. Perhaps our relationship with Him is new or untested and we don't yet have a photo album of family life we can flip through to remind us of His guiding presence in our life.

That's why trust is a risk. We never learn whether someone is worthy of our trust unless we risk walking with him. And that's exactly what God invites us to do: "Oh, taste and see that the LORD is good," David says, "blessed is the man who trusts in Him!" (Psalm 34:8, NKJV). God wants us to give Him a taste test.

A TRUSTWORTHY GUIDE WILL PASS THE TASTE TEST

In 1993 I learned that a taste test is a good way to find out if a guide is trustworthy. That's the year I flexed my trust muscle with a new kind of guide—you know, one of the canine variety—a Seeing Eye dog!

I was very naive when the process began. I assumed that I'd get a dog that would be smarter than most humans I know. I figured that he'd be so well trained that we'd go to the mall; I'd say, "Forward! Fifty-percent-off rack"; and he'd take me there. What I didn't realize was that I was going to be trained as much as the dog, if not more so.

I went to Southeastern Guide Dog Training School and

stayed for a month. On the first day there, I met Jim, the trainer, who told me that he tried to match each dog with just the right person. Using the harness that would eventually sit on the back of my guide dog, Jim took me on what he called a "Juno walk." He held on to one end of the harness and I held on to the other, and as we walked around the school campus, he tested the pace of my walk and the strength of my pull.

Jim also asked me lots of questions. He wanted to know about my family, my temperament, my schedule, my activities. When I told him that I traveled frequently to speak and sing, he took special note. I mentioned that I needed a dog with exceptional bladder control because I spend a lot of time in airports—which usually don't have portable puppy potties. He asked for a copy of one of my CDs, and later he took it to the kennel and played it for the dogs. I guess he wanted to make sure that none of them howled at the sound of my voice!

By the next day, Jim had chosen our dogs. He led a boisterous line of canines into the large room where we all waited. "Okay," he said, "I'm going to call your name, and then your dog's name. Then you call your dog."

I felt a thrill of anticipation. This dog represented a new form of freedom and mobility for me. He or she would be my constant companion and trusted guide. I figured that after the walk and all the questions, this would be a match made in heaven. I've had girlfriends who didn't go to that much trouble in choosing a husband!

Roll call began.

"Elizabeth," Jim said, "call your dog. His name is London." *What a classy name,* I thought. *Sounds sleek and sophisticated.*

"Deborah, call your dog. His name is Shoney." *What a cute name! Shoney must be bouncy and energetic.*

"Jeremy, call your dog. His name is Recon." *Now that's a studly name if I ever heard one!*

Jim called out ten more names. Each was creative and fun. Not a Fido in the bunch!

At last it was my turn. "Jennifer," Jim said, "call your dog. His name is [drum roll, please]…William." *William? What kind of name is that for a dog? A great name for a senator, maybe. But for a guide dog?*

Well, now I had a guide dog: William Rothschild. I only wish his behavior had been as dignified as his name. But it wasn't. He was loyal, but he had a problem—a besetting sin, you might say. William had a food distraction. In dogspeak that means the people who raised him fed him people food. Having tasted the finer things of life, whenever William was around people food, he wanted it so badly that he became totally distracted. Instead of focusing on me and my commands, he fixed his attention on the forbidden fodder just beyond his paws.

Let's just make sure you understand the scenario: Guide dogs go where people go. So in William's case, restaurants,

food courts at malls, and hotel banquet rooms were all set-
tings for potential disaster.

I realized that a food distraction was a pretty serious deal
one afternoon when William and I joined the class on a field
trip to McDonald's. Proudly, the members of the class
entered the restaurant one at a time with their dogs. When
it was our turn, William and I stood in the doorway, and I
gave him the command: "Forward." He hesitated. I'd been
taught that when a guide dog hesitates, I should check in
front of us for an obstruction. There might be a table or a
stair in front of me. Since William could recognize poten-
tially hazardous outcomes like falling down stairs or banging
into tables, he had been taught to simply stop when he
sensed danger. This is called "intelligent disobedience," and
it's one of the amazing features of guide dogs.

I checked in front of us. No table, no step, no obstruction—no reason for disobedience. So I issued another command. This time when I said "Forward, William," I added
an arm gesture, which he recognized as "Move it, buddy!"
Finally, he moved. But unfortunately, he did not move forward. Carrying me along with him, he bounded toward the
left side of the restaurant, where he landed in a booth with
his paws on the table. Then, looking like a happy, furry
human, he proceeded to scarf down the french fries of the
lady pinned next to him in the booth.

Listening to the screams of the terrified woman, I stood
there in disbelief, still strapped to that food-obsessed canine

with french fries hanging out of his mouth. When I managed to regain my composure, I used all my strength to pull William down from the table. Then I commanded him to sit, cupped his ketchup-smeared muzzle in my hand, and made him look me straight in the eye.

Those of you who follow the political scene will understand this next part. Early in the Clinton administration, there was extensive media coverage of the president's affection for fast food. So I looked in William's eyes and said, "From this day on, I call you Bill." Then I whistled "Hail to the Chief" as we marched off.

You've probably guessed that Bill and I had a little more training after that. When Jim realized just how serious the food distraction was, he suggested that we do morning doughnut walks. Sounds like a stroll through paradise, doesn't it? Well, believe me, it wasn't!

Every morning at 7:00 A.M., Bill and I would begin the doughnut drill. After I placed a special correction collar around his neck, we would proceed to walk. To our left, the sidewalk was dotted with small white powdered doughnuts, and the air was fragrant with the smell of the proscribed treat.

If Bill so much as looked at those doughnuts, I would immediately pull up on his leash...and *zing!* His correction collar would remind him to focus on me instead of on the doughnuts. We walked back and forth every day for a week, and it worked. Bill's behavior was definitely modified.

Pavlov would have been proud! It was so effective that I still can't eat a doughnut without getting a little bit uncomfortable around my collar.

As I risked walking with William and we forged a relationship, I learned what makes a guide trustworthy. After some more time and testing, he eventually proved to me that he had my best interest and safety at heart, and I came to trust him.

It could have been different. William could have failed the test and stayed focused on those doughnuts. Our God, however, always passes the taste test. "The LORD is good, a refuge in times of trouble. He cares for those who trust in him" (Nahum 1:7). With everything that's going on in the universe, He still remains focused on us. Everything He has done through the ages reflects that.

In the Garden, He pursued us.

In the ark, He protected us.

In the wilderness, He provided for us.

And on the cross, He proved to us that He alone is worthy of ultimate trust.

FEELINGS AREN'T TRUSTWORTHY GUIDES

Because God is trustworthy, what He says is also trustworthy. "In the beginning was the Word," says John, "and the Word was with God, and the Word was God" (John 1:1). It is impossible to separate who God is from what He says.

The psalmist says that God's Word is "a lamp to my feet

and a light for my path" (Psalm 119:105). There will be times when your path will be dark, times when you'll desperately need a light to guide you. When life's shadows hide Him from your view, you'll need the light of His promise that He will "never leave you nor forsake you" (Joshua 1:5). When life's circumstances rob you of your sense of security, you'll need the beacon of His assurance that He "knows what you need before you ask him" (Matthew 6:8). We can trust what God says to guide us when life is dark because He can see better than we can. "A man's ways are in full view of the LORD, and he examines all his paths" (Proverbs 5:21).

So why *don't* we allow His Word to guide us?

Why *don't* we trust the promises in the Bible?

I think it's because we trust our feelings more than we trust what God tells us.

Feelings are tough obstacles to overcome, aren't they? They seem so immediate and real. But we can learn to trust in spite of them. How? By looking at Someone who had it figured out and imitating Him.

Jesus knew what it was like to feel human because although He was fully God, He was also fully man. When He came to earth for us, He clothed Himself in humanity:

Being in very nature God, [He] did not consider equality with God something to be grasped, but made himself nothing, taking the very nature of a servant, being made in human likeness. And being found in appearance as a man, he humbled himself and became obedient to death—even death on a cross! (Philippians 2:6–8)

Does this mean that Jesus struggled with His feelings just as you and I do?

Yes, He did.

Emotions accompany all the events of our lives. If you have a broken relationship, chances are you'll feel sad or rejected. If your spouse dies, you'll likely feel lonely. If you're unjustly accused, you'll probably feel angry. The more importance you assign to the event, the more intensely you'll feel the emotion. So when Christ approached the most important event in His life, He did so with an intense emotion.

The Bible calls it *shame*.

"For the joy set before Him [He] endured the cross, despising the shame, and has sat down at the right hand of the throne of God" (Hebrews 12:2, NASB).

What really strikes me in this passage is a word that appears before *shame*. It is a word that graphically describes how Jesus dealt with His strong emotion. The word is translated several different ways, depending on the version. One says that Christ *scorned* the shame; another that He *despised* the shame. But in the original Greek, the word is *kataphroneo*. (Now, indulge me here! These are five foreign syllables that will help build your trust muscle!) *Kataphroneo* means "to consider with disregard" or "to esteem lowly."

What an awesome example Jesus gave us! He had feelings of shame, but He held them in low esteem.

What we hold in high esteem will eventually govern us, but what we hold in low esteem, *we* will govern. Yes, we need to acknowledge our feelings, but we should never regard them more highly than God's Word. Don't ever bow to your feelings because you hold them in such high regard. Instead, make them bow to your God.

Often we can't choose the feelings we experience. But we can always choose our *response* to them. We don't have to allow our feelings to dictate our choices. It may seem risky at the time, but if we don't esteem God's eternal Word more highly than we do our fleeting human feelings, we'll miss the blessings that wait on the other side of choosing to trust. Paul tells us what happened when Jesus esteemed God's Word more than His feelings and, in obedience to it, went to the cross:

> Therefore God exalted him to the highest place and gave him the name that is above every name, that at the name of Jesus every knee should bow, in heaven and on earth and under the earth, and every tongue confess that Jesus Christ is Lord, to the glory of God the Father. (Philippians 2:9–11)

Recently a lady at a conference told me that even though her friend Susan had wanted to attend, she wouldn't come with her. Susan has the same handicap I do. "Her husband is her eyes," her friend said. "She won't go anywhere without him." Since Susan thought her husband would feel out of place at a conference for women, she chose to stay home.

Why wouldn't Susan let her friend be her eyes for the day? A lack of trust? What keeps us from truly trusting? When I think about what keeps me from trusting, I realize that it's a feeling of fear that makes me unwilling to risk. But why did Jesus risk everything at the cross? *For the joy that was set before Him.* And what was His reward? *To sit down at the right hand of the throne of God.* The bigger the risk, the bigger the blessing! Who knows what blessings Susan missed because she was afraid to trust her friend?

A lot of us are that way and don't even realize it. When we say that we trust Him yet never risk acting upon His Word, we really don't trust Him at all. Trust shows itself when it leaves the tip of our tongue and lands on our tennis shoes. We begin to walk our faith, not just talk it.

Yes, of course we all feel afraid at times. It comes with the territory in our fallen human nature. But we can risk the frightening discomfort in order to find that we really can trust God. To trust Him fully means that we believe Him and act upon what He says. And when we do, His Word really does illuminate our path.

FEAR IS A FEELING; TRUST IS A CHOICE

Feeling fearful is a natural reaction to many of life's circumstances, but trust is always a supernatural choice.

The terrorist attacks on September 11, 2001, left all Americans reeling. In the aftermath, threats to airlines were a daily reality, and I struggled with the same feelings of fear as everyone else. My calendar, however, had been booked for a year, and I was scheduled to fly every weekend after September 11. A traveling companion who was scheduled to accompany me on several trips suddenly had to cancel when her husband was called to military duty.

That meant that I had to make several trips in a row by myself.

And I must admit that I was fearful.

The atmosphere in airports and airplanes was tense, and I was not looking forward to being alone. At least a companion could help me know what was happening and what to do if there was a problem.

I remember getting on my knees before God and telling Him that I was afraid. Immediately, this verse came to my mind: "When I am afraid, I will trust in you" (Psalm 56:3).

God knows that sometimes fear and trust share the same heartbeat. As I meditated on the verse, I suddenly realized that *I am afraid* describes a condition and that *I will trust* describes a volition. The verse is definitive: My volition can change my condition. For example, if *I am down*, but *I will get up*, my choice will change my situation. So if *I am afraid*, yet *I will trust*, my choice to trust God will inevitably change my feeling of fear.

When I resolved to trust God and fly, I flew without fear. Then I could quote with confidence what Paul told Timothy: "God has not given us a spirit of fear" (2 Timothy 1:7, NKJV).

It's true—He hasn't. So what has He given us?

The verse goes on to say that He has given us a spirit "of power and of love and of a sound mind." It is *God's* power in us—not our own—that gives us the ability to triumph over fear. The Bible also tells us that "perfect love drives out fear" (1 John 4:18) and that having a sound mind—taking captive every thought to make it obedient to Christ—can "demolish arguments and every pretension that sets itself up against the knowledge of God" (2 Corinthians 10:5). That includes fear.

Choosing to trust God gives us the resources we need to cast out fear. Yet ironically, fear can also help us trust God. How? By making us wise.

Through the years I've heard people talk about how much courage I must have. I'm amused by their comments. There's a line in a popular song to the effect that underneath a warrior's armor, you'll find a child. Isn't that a tender picture of someone fearlessly pursuing a life of trusting our Father? Well, here's another picture for you: Underneath this warrior's armor, you'll find a chicken. That's right! A grade-A, yellow-bellied, lily-livered chicken! It's scary walking through life in the dark.

Still, I would rather use fear wisely than foolishly waste it. So I'm learning to keep my feelings in check and exercise the kind of fear that will fuel my faith. The Bible says, "The fear of the LORD is the beginning of wisdom" (Psalm 111:10). Having a healthy reverence for God allows us to view our fears from the perspective of His mighty throne, and the wisdom that's born out of a genuine respect for Him gives us the discernment to gauge what is truly worth fearing.

Wisdom wears the garment of trust and walks without fear. Solomon said, "Wisdom is more precious than rubies, and nothing you desire can compare with her" (Proverbs 8:11). And God is willing to give us wisdom just for the asking!

When I was thirteen, I memorized James 1:5: "If any of you lacks wisdom, he should ask God, who gives generously to all without finding fault, and it will be given to him." I trusted God enough to ask. So when anyone marvels at my apparent "courage," I attribute it to my trusting prayer for wisdom. God has taught me to lovingly fear Him, and as a result, little else is really worth fearing. When we fear God most of all, trusting Him will be our wisest choice.

Even when life gets dark and scary.

Who among you fears the LORD and
obeys the word of his servant?
Let him who walks in the dark, who has no light,
trust in the name of the LORD and rely on his God.

ISAIAH 50:10

Be Thou My Vision

Be Thou my Vision, O Lord of my heart
Naught be all else to me, save that Thou art
Thou my best thought, by day or by night
Waking or sleeping, Thy presence my light

Riches I heed not, nor man's empty praise
Thou mine Inheritance, now and always
Thou and Thou only, first in my heart
High King of heaven, my Treasure Thou art

High King of heaven, my victory won
May I reach heaven's joys, O bright heaven's Sun!
Heart of my own heart, whatever befall
Still be my Vision, O Ruler of all

EIGHTH-CENTURY IRISH POEM TRANSLATED BY MARY BYRNE VERSIFIED BY ELEANOR HULL

Three

REMEMBER *What* MATTERS

〜

Here's a question for you: What do these ten things have in common?

1. a ballpoint pen
2. a bicycle
3. a snowman
4. a Volkswagen bug
5. a five-dollar bill
6. a monkey's tail
7. a golf club
8. a pair of glasses
9. a submarine periscope
10. ten little Indians

On the surface they don't seem to have much of anything in common—but you might be surprised! Each item on the list contains a symbol, and each symbol represents a number. Assigning a symbol and a number to things is the way I memorize grocery and to-do lists.

I learned how to do this when I was a junior in college. One day my psychology professor asked each of the forty students in our class to name any item he or she chose. After the fortieth person added something, I listened in astonishment as the professor began to tick off everything on the list—in perfect order. Next he challenged us to call out numbers at random, and he then proceeded to connect each one with the correct item. It was amazing!

Inspired by that demonstration, I vowed to learn to remember just like he did. To remember the items on this list, for example, I would imagine number 1 with a ballpoint stuck in it, number 2 riding on the seat of a bike, or a monkey swinging by his tail from number 6. That's pretty much the technique. I mastered it, and now if you ask me to remember a list, almost all of the time I can.

For me, memory is more reliable than sight. One of the oddities of living with failing sight is that the changes are often sudden, yet subtle. Many times I've operated on the mistaken notion that I could see where I was going, only to realize—when I walked into a wall—that my sight had worsened. If I had made it a point to remember where the doorway was, I would have made it safely down the hall.

In a spiritual sense, that's true for all of us. As we're learning to trust God and walk by faith, we also need to learn to remember His Word. That's because knowing what God tells us in the Bible helps us to act upon what we *know* is true, rather than merely reacting to what we see.

Life presents us with many optical illusions. Have you ever been in the desert and seen that tantalizing shoreline of water shimmering on the horizon? You could chase it all your life and never wet so much as your big toe. It isn't really there! And that's often true with what we think we're seeing so clearly. The information provided by our eyes may simply be unreliable. There are also times when we can't see at all. So we must memorize the truth and make sure we remember what matters.

SOMETHING TO KEEP IN MIND

One cold January afternoon, our family had just returned to Springfield, Missouri, after a long, tiring drive. Before going home, we had to stop at the store, and as we pulled into the parking lot, it was all I could do to wait for the car to stop before I opened the door. The heat in our van had abandoned us about three hours from home, and I was cold! As soon as Phil shut off the engine, I swung the door open and held on as it pulled me swiftly out of the van. By the time Phil and our oldest son, Clayton, had opened their doors, I was headed to the middle of the parking lot.

"Stop, Mom," Clayton yelled. "There's a car coming!"

Phil ran over to me. "Why are you in such a hurry?" he asked.

Before I could answer, Clayton said, "Mom, you could have been hit by a car. That would've been awful!"

I was pleased with his concern and ashamed of my impetuousness. "You're right," I said. "That would have been awful."

"Yeah," Clayton said. "Because if you died, Dad and I would *never* be able to find anything!"

Well, that was about the most accurate statement I'd ever heard!

My guys are fully sighted, but I'm still their eyes. They're constantly asking me, "Where's my…?" and "Have you seen my…?" Since they don't pay any attention to where they put things, it's easier for them to ask me than it is to search. Clayton feared that if I died, he and his dad would never find anything because they rely heavily on my memory to find their stuff for them.

My world is pretty dark, so I must depend on my memory. If something is out of its place, I can't access it, and it's as though it doesn't exist. I have to diligently maintain my closet, my pantry, and my refrigerator because I can't rely on others to find the chocolate chips when my hormones are screaming, "Feed me! Feed me!" And that's only the beginning. There are so many things I have to order and organize in my life—knowing that I can't always rely on someone being there to check it out for me visually. Do my socks match when I leave the house in the morning? They do if I've put them in the right place! I must rely completely on remembering where things are and maintaining good habits to keep them in the places I've memorized.

Relying on sight is okay...as long as we can see. But what if the electricity goes out? Let's face it: We all have times when life gets dark, times when we just can't see. To shed light on our path, we have to know God's Word. The psalmist put it this way: "I will delight in your principles and not forget your word" (Psalm 119:16, NLT).

None of us can be certain that we'll have access to a Bible just when we need it, and we can't rely solely on others, like our pastor or Bible-study teacher, to find the exact Scripture we need. If we don't discipline ourselves to memorize the truth, it won't be accessible when we reach for it. That means we must sear the Word into our gray matter. We must learn to remember the Scripture that will guide us when we can't see.

Suppose one day a job layoff, a car accident, or a serious illness shakes your tranquil world. Life suddenly seems mercilessly dark. But if you have memorized the truth that God will keep in perfect peace those whose minds are stayed on Him (Isaiah 26:3), you will react peacefully based on what you know to be true.

Is there a darkness threatening you? Try to identify it, and then memorize what God says about your situation.

Here are some examples from the New Century Version of the Bible:

- Is it fear? Remember Matthew 10:29–31: "Two sparrows cost only a penny, but not even one of them can die without your Father's knowing it.... So don't be afraid. You are worth much more than many sparrows."

- Is it loneliness? Remember Hebrews 13:5: "God has said, 'I will never leave you; I will never forget you.'"

- Is it guilt? Remember 2 Corinthians 5:17: "If anyone belongs to Christ, there is a new creation. The old things have gone; everything is made new!"

- Is it worry? Remember 1 Peter 5:7: "Give all your worries to [God], because he cares about you."

- Is it getting older? Remember Isaiah 46:4: "Even when you are old, I will be the same. Even when your hair has turned gray, I will take care of you."

- Is it disappointment? Remember Matthew 5:4: "Those who are sad now are happy, because God will comfort them."

Memorizing the truth will allow the Light of the World to illuminate even your darkest places with the radiance of His Word. If you remember what matters, a good memory will see you through.

MEMORIES THAT MATTER

When I was a little girl, long before my eyes grew dim, I used to lie upon the grass in my front yard and gaze at the sky. The sun always fell softly on my skin on those warm Florida afternoons. As I stretched out under the silk oak tree and gazed at the billows of white in the clear blue sky, the clouds would become images in my imagination. I could see hammers and elves. Trucks and teapots. Once I raced into the house to proudly announce that I had seen Snow White and all seven dwarfs.

At times I still gaze heavenward into that vast blue canvas stretched out overhead, but now, even on the most brilliant days, all my eyes see is gray. Sometimes that makes me feel sad—until I remember the clouds. They still dance through my imagination to the music only my memory can hear. Then I smile, for I have a treasure hidden in my memory that no eye disease can ever touch. I can stretch out in the front yard with my two sons and enjoy the pictures the clouds draw for them.

Memory will sustain you even when sight won't serve you. That's why it's essential to remember what really matters. It's important to remember the clouds.

The Bible says that when the children of Israel were in the wilderness, God "guided them with the cloud by day and with light from the fire all night" (Psalm 78:14). I bet the nation of Israel remembered the cloud that led them. But I also bet that when they remembered the cloud, they couldn't help but recall the difficulties of their journey through the wilderness. The desert was a place of longing and need, a place that required them to depend totally upon God.

Why did God allow His covenant people to wander in the desert for so long? The Old Testament suggests that it was because the harsh conditions of the wilderness revealed the true nature of the sojourners. Early in the book of Exodus we begin to read accounts of grumbling and complaints on the part of the Israelites. Their faith grew faint, and they often lost their perspective. Later, Moses reminded them about that: "Remember how the LORD your God led you through the wilderness for forty years, humbling you and testing you to prove your character, and to find out whether or not you would really obey his commands" (Deuteronomy 8:2, NLT).

I believe that God allows all of us to wander through deserts at times in order to test us. The wilderness shows who we really are and whom we really trust. Sometimes God lets us be hungry just so He can feed us, and sometimes He lets us wander just so we'll look for Him in the cloud.

So when you think of your desert, remember the cloud. In the Old Testament it always represents God's presence. When the Israelites' journey through the wilderness was over, they still faced an uncertain future across the Jordan, and they were afraid. But even though the cloud was no longer there to guide them, God was still there. "The LORD himself goes before you and will be with you," Moses reminded them; "he will never leave you nor forsake you. Do not be afraid; do not be discouraged" (Deuteronomy 31:8).

Even when clouds darken our world, if we look closely, we'll see that He is with us, and His presence will always lead us to our promised land.

Remember what matters.

If you do, you'll never forget in the dark what you knew was true in the light, and you'll be able to smile even when you see nothing but gloomy shadows. Remembering what really matters, however, takes some memory maintenance.

That Reminds Me

Okay. I'm sure you've already asked yourself—especially the ladies—*How in the world does she put on makeup?* Someday—in the middle of a massive power blackout—that might become an issue of paramount importance for you. So I'll let you in on my secret.

I do it through concentration and reinforcement.

My mother taught me the system years ago, and over time I've adjusted it slightly to accommodate style and fashion. It all involves counting. I know just how many times to brush my blush brush against my blush palette (I dare you to read that out loud three times fast!) and exactly where and how many times to swish that brush along my cheekbone. The system works the same for eyeliner, mascara, lipliner, and eye shadow. It's very reliable as long as I concentrate and don't lose count. In fact, it's more reliable than looking in a mirror. If you make it a habit, you can apply your makeup during a full solar eclipse!

But here's the catch: My system for putting on makeup is only as reliable as my ability to *reinforce* what I have memorized. Sure, I know just how many strokes and swishes it takes to make myself over, but if I didn't habitually practice what I've memorized, I'd soon forget. And the result wouldn't be pretty!

Well, guess what? The result of allowing truths we've memorized to be forgotten due to mental laziness isn't pretty either. The psalmist says, "Your Word I have treasured in my heart, that I may not sin against You" (Psalm 119:11, NASB).

Still, the truths we find in God's Word are far more than precepts that help us not to sin; in and of themselves they are treasures worth preserving. All throughout Psalm 119, the writer says "I will remember" and "I do not forget."

And guess what he's referring to?

God's Word.

He knew the value of remembering it. Look at some of the things that are ours when we hide it in our heart:

- God's Word is our counselor. (v. 24)
- God's Word strengthens us. (v. 28)
- God's Word is our delight. (v. 35)

- God's Word comforts us in our affliction. (v. 52)
- God's Word makes us wiser than our enemies. (v. 98)
- God's Word gives us more insight than our teachers. (v. 99)
- God's Word is sweet to our mouths. (v. 103)
- God's Word gives us understanding. (v. 104)
- God's Word renews our lives. (v. 156)
- God's Word gives us peace. (v. 165)

See what a precious treasure you have in God's Word? Treat it like the treasure it is and hide it in your heart. Write it upon the tablet of your memory, and to maintain it frequently, review what you've memorized.

There are a number of ways to reinforce your memory. One of the things I do to help me not forget and keep my Scripture memory agile is to take my cues from the clock. Here's what I mean. If I'm sitting down to hot tea and sugar cookies in the afternoon, I press my talking watch. If it says 3:23, I immediately think of a verse with that address. Ah, Romans 3:23, "For all have sinned and fall short of the glory of God." Or perhaps Colossians 3:23, "Whatever you do, work at it with all your heart, as working for the Lord, not for men."

If I can't quote the verse, I get out my Bible on tape, look it up, and work on reciting it. If I can't think of any address that corresponds with the time, I try to find one. Our family also uses Scripture cards at the dinner table. We read one each night and take turns practicing reciting it.

These are just two ways to maintain what we've memorized. We can memorize anything if we concentrate on it and reinforce it. Then it becomes near to us, and we act upon what we have memorized. "The word is very near you, in your mouth and in your heart, that you may do it" (Deuteronomy 30:14, NKJV). If we can do it with cosmetics, we can certainly do it with the Word!

Now that I've told you my secret of applying makeup, I want to let you in on a Rothschild family secret for applying Scripture.

It's our personal family code. It consists of two numbers, and it contains all we need to have a power-packed day. The two numbers are 4 and 13.

When Clayton leaves for school in the morning, I'll call out, "4:13."

When I'm feeling overwhelmed, Clayton will respectfully say, "4:13 it, Mom."

When Phil has a major project due at work, I'll remind him, "4:13, honey."

When Connor has a toddler meltdown in the candy aisle at the grocery store, I...*pay four dollars and thirteen cents to the cashier just to get him to be quiet!*

Just kidding!

You may have already guessed that 4:13 stands for the well-known and much beloved Scripture in Philippians, "I can do all things through Christ who strengthens me" (NKJV). For us, that verse is an awesome reminder that with the power and presence of Christ in our lives, nothing, but nothing, is too big, too hard, too puzzling, or too overwhelming to warrant an "I can't" attitude.

Corrie ten Boom's family had a secret, too. When they were arrested by Hitler's regime, the family members whispered to one another, "What do you have in your shoe, Corrie?" "What do you have in your shoe, Daddy?" "What do you have in your shoe, Betsy?"

What was in their shoes? Romans 8, Ephesians 1, and 2 Corinthians 4. According to Corrie, they had torn pages of Scripture from their Bibles and placed them in the soles of their shoes. Talk about *standing* on the promises! Even while they were confined to a concentration camp and enduring harsh conditions of hunger and abuse, they knew they were walking with the Word.

When we have memorized God's Word, it becomes real to us—it becomes what we speak and what we stand on—and it empowers us to do all things through Christ, regardless of our circumstance. So learn to remember His Word. Speak it to yourself and to those around you. Stand firmly upon it. May it be written on your soles and penetrate your soul.

You shall put these words of mine in your heart and
soul, and you shall bind them as a sign on your hand,

and fix them as an emblem on your forehead. Teach
them to your children, talking about them when you
are at home and when you are away, when you lie
down and when you rise. (Deuteronomy 11:18–19,
NRSV)

Never forget that the important things sealed in your
memory are never lost. So spend time memorizing what
matters, and maintain what you have memorized. When it's
dark and you can't see, God will become your vision if His
truths are hidden in your heart.

Most of all, remember the Lord, for He never forgets
you. You are always on His mind and in His thoughts. He
remembers what matters—you! So by day or by night, make
Him your best thought, and make sure you always remember to thank Him for His Word and His goodness to you.

Remember His wonders which He has done,
His marvels and the judgments uttered by His mouth.

PSALM 105:5, NASB

Matchless Grace

Just when I need You most, You hear me
Just when I least deserve, You rescue me
All of the times I've failed You
Just show Your promises to be true

Matchless grace, oh how kind
That in Your heart You would find
Matchless grace to forgive
And to lend the strength to live
By matchless grace

All of my earthly strength is weakness
My soul depends on You for completeness
It's by Your grace that I am
And by Your grace that I will stand

Matchless grace, oh how kind
That in Your heart You would find
Matchless grace to forgive
And to lend the strength to live
By matchless grace

WORDS AND MUSIC BY JENNIFER ROTHSCHILD © 1990 ROTHSCHILD MUSIC (ASCAP)

Four

RECEIVE GOD'S GIFTS *with* THANKS

~

D o you remember the robot in the 1970s TV show *Lost in Space?* Most of the time when he showed up, his arms waved and his lights flashed a warning: "Danger! Danger!" That's what I often feel like—as though my blindness somehow sends a silent signal that says "Warning: Danger!"

Most women can call a friend and say, "Let's go shopping." It's simple and straightforward. But if I call a friend to make the same suggestion, I fear that what she really hears is "Will you come pick me up, lead me around the store, pick out clothes, read the labels to me, and then be my mirror? After that, will you place my pen on the line so I can sign for my purchase, and then will you drive me home and walk me into the house?"

It's kind of like having to get a toddler in and out of a car seat while you run errands. It's not that you don't love the child's company; it's just that it's so much easier to go alone. That's how I feel in a lot of my friendships—loved and enjoyed, yet a complicating factor in someone's otherwise uncomplicated world. That feeling makes me stare at my blindness and decide if I'm going to gratefully receive it as a gift from God and become a better person, or despise it and become a bitter one.

The only difference between becoming *bitter* and becoming *better* is the letter *I*. Approaching our difficulties from the standpoint of what *I* want, what *I* have lost, or what *I* think is fair will embitter us. Bitter eyes can perceive only the injustice and the sorrow in our situation. Grateful eyes, however, will always see the grace of God, regardless of how difficult our circumstances might be. Grateful eyes allow us to see "the goodness of the LORD in the land of the living" (Psalm 27:13).

Even though blindness has been a difficult gift to receive, I now can accept it with thanks. As I've learned to view my circumstances from God's perspective, I've learned to gratefully receive.

DIFFICULT GIFTS

One reason many people struggle with bitterness and ungratefulness is that they've never learned to receive difficult gifts. Blindness is just one of many such gifts. Illness, broken relationships, wayward children, and financial strain can be very hard to receive, much less be thankful for. But the interesting thing is that God expects us to be thankful anyway. "Give thanks in all circumstances," the apostle Paul reminds us, "for this is God's will for you in Christ Jesus" (1 Thessalonians 5:18).

I vividly remember the night before Christmas when I was nine years old. One of our family traditions was that each child got to open one gift on Christmas Eve. My brothers and I spent most of the month deciding which gift that would be. We began our research in early December, and as each gift appeared beneath the tree, we carefully examined it, checking the weight and shape of each box, looking for clues to what was inside. As you can well imagine, by Christmas Eve the gift we had chosen to open had become the most coveted one under the tree.

That year my brother Lawson and I both chose a gift from Aunt Patti. (Our brother David was a baby and still too young to care.) Aunt Patti was young and hip. She knew what kinds of presents kids liked, and now she joined my parents on the couch to watch the events unfold.

Lawson went first. He carefully removed the wrappings—and there was a brand-new GI Joe action figure. It had been on his list, so, boy, was he excited! I was excited, too, because it confirmed my hopeful suspicion that my gift from Aunt Patti was the number one thing on my wish list—a Barbie doll.

My gift was in a rectangular-shaped box. It wasn't the traditional box that a Barbie doll came in, but it was *shaped* like one, and I was convinced that Aunt Patti was just trying to fool me. I pulled off the narrow rectangular top, peeled back the tissue paper—and there were seven pairs of neatly rolled underwear.

Underwear! I wanted a Barbie doll, not underwear. I didn't even care if I wore underwear. My mother obviously noticed my disappointment because without hesitation, she said, "Jennifer, what do you say to Aunt Patti?"

"Thank you," I said.

Now, why did I say thank you for a gift that I hadn't asked for and obviously didn't want? Because from as early as I could remember, my mother had taught me that I was always to receive whatever anyone gave me and say thank you for it. She had instilled in me how important it is to always honor the giver by gratefully receiving the gift. So one reason for saying thank you was to honor Aunt Patti. Another was that it was my mother's will—and I knew that I would be a lot happier if I obeyed her!

Being thankful in all circumstances shows that we're acting in accordance with the will of God—who always gives us what is best for us. Often we struggle with an attitude of ungratefulness because our eyes are fixed so fiercely on the gift. Some things that God allows to come into our lives are genuinely hard to be thankful for. But if we fix our eyes on God, we can see beyond the difficulty of the gift into the heart of the Giver. Regardless of whether we asked for it or want it, it's a gift of God's grace, and our response should always be to receive it with thanks.

Is your response to a difficult gift based on your feelings about the gift itself or on your desire to honor the Giver and do His will? Is your closed fist extended in anger, or is your open hand lifted to Him? Only an open hand receives the blessings that accompany difficult gifts, and sometimes it's only in a package wrapped in heartache that we receive the fullness of God's grace.

Faith is the most essential ingredient for gratefully receiving whatever God lovingly allows, and it can be the greatest source of blessing in our lives when we learn to see what it sees. But to do that, we have to look at our lives from the right perspective.

THE RIGHT PERSPECTIVE

Connor had a new balloon and insisted on taking it to the backyard.

"Connor," I told him, "if we take the balloon out in the backyard it will probably get popped."

But he would not relent, so out we went. He swept the brightly colored balloon up into the air, and it slowly glided downward. He caught it and repeated the motion several times. Up, down; up, down. Eventually, the balloon lifted and dropped earthward for its final descent. He didn't catch it. *Pop!* Bits of wrinkly red rubber dotted the grass. With stunning composure, Connor gathered the tattered pieces in his chubby hands and ran toward me.

"Mommy," he said, "fix it!"

Why didn't that little guy fall apart over the demise of his beloved balloon? Because of his perspective. Although the reality was that the balloon couldn't be fixed, little Connor's perspective on life was still *Mommy can fix anything.* His confident response to the situation was based less on reality itself than on the way he perceived it.

Sometimes you and I find ourselves on the brink of a spiritual meltdown when the reality we face is hard. But I believe that our perspective on our adversity can often be more powerful than the hardship itself. If beauty is in the eye of the beholder, so is pain and heartache.

I remember a creative writing class I took years ago. "I want everyone to stare at this chalkboard and imagine that it's a window," the professor announced, "and then write an essay about what you see through it." Pens began to dance on crisp, white paper, and after forty-five minutes the teacher called for volunteers to read what they had written.

One not-so-deep thinker gave mind-numbing details of the Bills versus Dolphins game he was watching through the window of his luxurious skybox. Another more imaginative writer saw through delicate snowflakes sticking to the glass to the ice-capped mountains on the other side of the window. Yet another saw the dark, mysterious cemetery that beckoned him to his father's grave.

Keep in mind that all we *really* saw was a plain old unattractive chalkboard. And sometimes it seems as though that's all life offers, doesn't it? Uninviting situations with no inherent beauty or appeal—just dusty gray slate. Hard stuff. But if seeing is a physical function of the eye, it's also a spiritual function of the soul, and what we see through the window of hardship depends on the perspective we choose. Like those creative writers, we need to choose how we will perceive it.

Shifting our gaze can help us. If we look around, we'll see bigger problems than our own. In moments when my blindness makes me feel frustrated and discouraged, I think of a man I know who lives and performs in Branson, Missouri. He is a gifted singer and plays the guitar masterfully—with his feet, for he was born without arms. I think about what his life must be like. Yes, he can drive a car, read a book, and see his surroundings. But he can't embrace his wife or hold his children. When I think about that, I begin to genuinely thank God for what I do have, because it's so much greater than what I've lost.

I'm not saying that we should dismiss our heartache as trivial because "someone else has it worse." The bottom line is that someone else will *always* have it worse, and we will *always* have heartache. I'm simply suggesting that shifting our gaze to a bigger problem will put our own situation in perspective—and prompt an attitude of gratefulness that will release us from the shackles of bitterness.

Sometimes, though, it's hard to look around for a bigger problem, because the one we're dealing with seems awfully big to us.

That's why we also need to look up.

As we shift our gaze heavenward, it becomes focused on God and His promises. "The LORD God is a sun and shield," writes the psalmist; "the LORD will give grace and glory: no good thing will he withhold from them that walk uprightly" (Psalm 84:11, KJV). When we choose to view our life from that perspective, our grateful eyes will see God's goodness all around us.

GRATEFUL EYES SEE GRACE AND GLORY

Before I lost my sight, my career goal was to be a commercial artist. I loved to draw! I had several years of lessons, and cartooning and lettering were my forte. I inherited my talent from my mother, who is quite the artist.

Mom had a special knack for training her children to perceive the subtle nuances of every color of the spectrum. It was rare for her to use less than five adjectives to describe a color.

I knew what red looked like when it was warm and orangey on the skin of a tomato. I knew what it was to see the beautiful blue undertones just beneath the red paint of a fire engine. I loved the color yellow, whether it was splashed upon an ear of corn or lying gently upon a buttercup. Even though my eyes no longer see color, every one I ever saw is still fresh and vibrant in my mind's eye. There I can still see all the hues of all the colors I saw when I was growing up.

How special it was for me, then, when one day Clayton came home from preschool and showed the same eye for color as his grandmother. He held a crumpled piece of paper toward me and said, "Mommy, look at this beautiful flower."

By the time he was three, Clayton had learned that in order for his mommy to see, he needed to use words. So he began to describe the picture of his beautiful flower. "Mommy," he said, "the flower is pink. And the leaves are not just green, they are a yellowish green."

I remember sitting on our front porch, holding the picture in my hand. I could have felt it stab me as a painful reminder that I would never draw again and never have the opportunity to enjoy art with my son. Instead, I felt amazed that Clayton's little eyes could perceive the difference between a bluish and a yellowish green.

That day it was as if God illustrated for me a beautiful picture of His goodness. It was as if I could see a shade of His grace I'd never seen before. And I think that I wouldn't have seen the beauty in that picture if God had not already taught me to have grateful eyes.

Grateful eyes see God's glory as well as His grace, and the glory of God is what turns all the pictures in our lives into beautiful works of art. Thumbing through the photo album of my life, I see many snapshots in my mind's eye, including one that at first glance doesn't seem very delightful to behold. But when I take a closer look through grateful eyes, I see it bathed in the radiance of God's glory.

One spring evening I arrived at a hotel in Destin, Florida, where I was to speak at a women's conference the following day. I didn't feel well at bedtime, but I assumed that I just needed a good night's sleep and that I'd be fine in the morning.

Boy, was I wrong! The next morning I was in severe pain. If I'd been pregnant, I would have assumed I was in labor. But I wasn't—and this was worse than labor! I ended up in the emergency room of the local hospital, where I quickly learned what kidney stones are.

Surgery took the place of my speaking engagement that night, and when I came out of the anesthetic, I was very discouraged. *Had I flown across the country just to be stuck in a hospital?* It was hard to be grateful for such a strange turn of events.

But then the words of Peter began running through my mind: "Dear friends, do not be surprised at the painful trial you are suffering, as though something strange were happening to you. But rejoice that you participate in the sufferings of Christ, so that you may be overjoyed when his glory is revealed" (1 Peter 4:12–13).

It was the very verse I was to have spoken on that night, and it encouraged me to go ahead and rejoice.

So I did.

Instead of thinking about the strange thing that had happened to me, I chose to be grateful and to settle into what God had allowed. I knew from Matthew 24:27 that someday Jesus would burst like lightning through the eastern sky and I'd see His glory. *And then,* I thought, *I'll be more than joyful—I'll be overjoyed.* What I didn't expect was that right then His glory was about to burst into my hospital room.

As I lay there, I heard a soft knock, quickly followed by the sound of a door opening.

"Jennifer," a female voice said, "you don't know me, but I work here, and I saw your name come up on my computer screen. You spoke several years ago at a conference I attended when I was battling breast cancer. God used you to help me, and—I had to come to say thank you. By the way, my name is Gloria."

Gloria.

And just like that, God's glory began to fill that hospital room. It was as though God shone a huge spotlight on that strange, painful *incident* in my life and turned it into a beautiful picture for the album of my life. I didn't have to wait until "someday" to see His glory revealed; His glory had walked right into my hospital room. As Gloria spoke words of encouragement and purpose, God's glory washed over my discouragement, allowing me to see His goodness.

I was overjoyed, not by the difficult circumstance, but by how God *used* it.

Do you see the distinction? It's so critical to let this truth seep into the roots of your heart. I'm convinced that God often wraps difficult gifts with His grace—and then uses them to display His glory. For that reason, we are the ones who truly benefit when we choose to gratefully receive them.

THE LONE LEPER

Often we assume that it would be easy to be grateful if God would simply *remove* the difficult gifts from our lives. Right? Nothing could be easier for Him. Then we would just naturally well up with feelings of gratitude that would overflow in praise to God. But believe me, the chances of that happening are slim. I struggled with statistics in college, but looking at Luke 17, even I can see that the odds are against us.

In fact, they're just one in ten.

Jesus was on His way to Jerusalem when ten lepers called out to Him to have pity on them. To put it mildly, those lepers had it very hard. The disease had ravaged and disfigured their bodies, and made them outcasts in a society that considered them unclean. So they cried out for Jesus to show them mercy, and He did. Then He told them to go show themselves to the priests.

One of the lepers, when he realized he had been healed, immediately came back to find Jesus. In verse 16, Luke says that the leper "threw himself at Jesus' feet and thanked him." Jesus asked the grateful man about the other nine. Where were they?

I wonder about them, too. Why didn't they return? Why didn't sheer gratitude catapult them back to Jesus? I wonder...until I look in the mirror and realize that centuries later I scurry through my busy life just like one of the nine. When I was eight years old, I received an unspeakable gift: the redemption of my soul. It came to me through a hand of mercy in the rugged wrappings of the Cross, and it has given me light in the darkness, water in the desert, and hope amid sorrow.

Yet sometimes I forget to return to say thank you. Like the nine heedless, forgetful ones, I hurry on my way, savoring the gift but forgetting all about the One who gave.

May we all be like the one, rather than the nine.

May we all be like the leper who exhibited his faith by choosing to give thanks.

We often think that faith is a recipe for getting what we want from God. If that were true, it would mean that if I could just muster enough faith, I would no longer be blind. But faith is not meant to offer an escape from life's difficulties; its purpose is to give us strength to endure them. God allows hardship because of His great mercy and love for us, and He often removes it for the same reason. However, we should not thank Him more fervently on the day our difficult gift is removed than we do on the days we carry it. It takes just as much faith to bear a burden as it does to believe that it can be removed.

Your faith shows itself in a response of thankfulness in all circumstances. Bitterness never kneels at God's throne; it just shakes an angry fist. Gratitude, however, like the lone leper, throws itself before Christ. When you smash the last brick of your wall of bitterness with the hammer of gratitude, you will hear the echo of the words Jesus spoke to the leper: "Your faith has made you well" (Luke 17:19).

Have you come back, thrown yourself at His feet, and thanked Him? Until you do, you'll never experience the wellness that your faith can provide.

To be reminded of God's great gift of salvation makes all other gifts pale in comparison. All of us who have received it need to come back to Jesus and throw ourselves before Him, praising and thanking Him loudly. When we learn to be truly grateful for His greatest gift, we'll learn to gratefully receive any other gift He may allow.

"You are worthy, our Lord and God,
to receive glory and honor and power, for you created all things,
and by your will they were created and have their being."

REVELATION 4:11

Rejoice in You

I will rejoice in You
God of my salvation
You always see me through
I will rejoice in You

Out of the darkness, into the light
Healed from blindness, given new sight
Walking in victory, power, and might
I am triumphant over the fight

When I rejoice in You
God of my salvation
You always see me through
I will rejoice in You

A song of deliverance now I can sing
Your love has conquered; death has no sting
New every morning mercies you bring
I shout it boldly, You are the King!

When I rejoice in You
God of my salvation
You always see me through
I will rejoice in You

WORDS AND MUSIC BY JENNIFER ROTHSCHILD © 1993 ROTHSCHILD MUSIC (ASCAP)

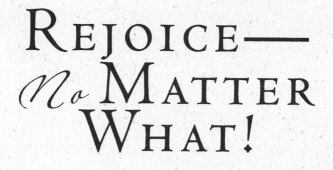

Five

REJOICE— *No* MATTER WHAT!

W e had just moved into our new home in Springfield. Our things were barely out of the boxes—and I was almost out of my mind!

That's no big surprise. Moving has been on the short list of top stressors since at least the 1960s. But it's especially stressful if you're blind.

Part of what makes life easier for a blind person is having an orderly world. Everything has a place, and everything must be in its place. But moving is the antithesis of an orderly world. At any given moment, chaos threatens to reign! Nothing has a place, and even if it did, it probably wouldn't be in it.

In order for me to know where everything is, I have to

unpack all the boxes, touch each item, and literally put it in its place. When I'm done, my kids can use me as their own personal tracking device. Why waste your energy searching the house for something when Mama's brain is equipped with GPS?

Finally, I was almost finished unpacking. Phil had helped me mark all the appliances with raised dots and tactile markings, and the kitchen was serviceable, so we graduated from delivered pizza to homemade lasagna. After I got it ready, I preheated the oven to 350 degrees and opened the door to put it in. First attempt...*ouch!* Second attempt... *ouch!* Third attempt...a very loud and unladylike *ouch!* I fought to get that lasagna in the oven, and I have the battle scars to prove it! (Yes, I should have learned the inside of the oven *before* it reached 350 degrees.)

As I nursed my wounds, I longed for my world to become orderly again. My stinging arms were a painful reminder of how difficult change can be. I didn't like having to adjust; I was tired of tripping over boxes and feeling my way around my new domain. "I'm tired of making adjustments, Lord," I cried. "I'm tired of having to unpack each box by hand just so I know where everything is. And I'm tired of all the bumps, bruises, and burns!"

No one heard me except God. *Whew!* It's a good thing, because I was already beginning to hear that violin tuning up to play dirges for my pity party. I don't think anyone else would have had much fun.

Sometimes it's good to let it all out…and I did. God is a patient listener. But there's a fine line between inviting God into our heartache and gearing up to send invitations for the "poor me" event of the year. In fact, nowhere does God tell us to throw pity parties. Instead, the Bible says: "Consider it pure joy, my brothers, whenever you face trials of many kinds" (James 1:2). If we think of a trial as joy, our response will be to rejoice.

James doesn't say to consider it joy *if* hardships come; he says to consider it joy *when* they come. They will come— that's just reality—and that means we'll certainly have opportunities to rejoice. All throughout the New Testament, we are told to rejoice in our trials. *Well, that's tough,* I thought, *learning to rejoice when our world heats up and life stings!*

That got me to thinking about what joy really is. One of the Hebrew words in the Old Testament that is translated as our English word *joy* means "a special goodness in the widest sense." When I realized that's what God intended this trial to be, I no longer wanted to whine and wither. I wanted to rejoice!

God's Word tells us not only what joy is, but also what happens when we learn to rejoice in our trials. Now there's a reason to strike up the band and throw a party!

A Discipline That Strengthens

When we rejoice in hardship, we acknowledge that God permits it for a purpose—to discipline us. I've got to tell you: *Discipline* is one of my least favorite words. I think the reason is because in the past I have misunderstood it. Parenting, however, has taught me that the true nature of discipline is not punishment but training.

I think that's God's view of discipline, too. His discipline is not to punish us, but to change us, and He allows suffering to be the hurdles we jump to strengthen us. He uses suffering to make us strong.

My friend Katharyn willingly subjects herself to the torture of running marathons. I don't know why. Personally, I enjoy running my mouth, running the dishwasher, and running to the mall. But running 26.2 miles? *Yikes!* Katharyn applies a lot of discipline and training in order to succeed in a marathon. Months in advance she wakes up before sunrise and starts to run. As the days progress, her route lengthens. Even though it's never easy, her training pays off. By the time of the marathon, she is lean, strong, and ready to race.

You should see her at the end of the race! She looks like someone ran her skinny body through the washing machine, bleached the color out of it, and then wrung it relentlessly until all that remained was wet, wrinkly, and worn.

But Katharyn really doesn't care what she looks like when she crosses the finish line at the end of the race. Her goal is to finish, and it's worth all the training just to cross that finish line.

Training and discipline are also the very things that

enable us to finish the race. Paul said, "I buffet my body" (1 Corinthians 9:27, ASV). In the American Standard Version of the Bible, you could easily mistake the verb in this verse for *buffet*—you know, like the midnight smorgasbord on a Carnival cruise. But no one can run well if they spend too much time doing that kind of "buffeting," so it's a good thing that's not what it means.

In the original Greek the word *buffet* actually means *to discipline by hardships.* A runner will discipline himself and endure arduous training in order to be fit for the race.

It's not easy. We can become weathered and weary. And even though discipline is intended to produce deep-seated character change, it can cause us pain, as the writer of Hebrews reminds us: "God disciplines us for our good, that we may share in his holiness. No discipline seems pleasant at the time, but painful. Later on, however, it produces a harvest of righteousness and peace for those who have been trained by it" (Hebrews 12:10–11).

God chooses to allow suffering to discipline us, yet it is our choice to discipline ourselves to respond with rejoicing. Both forms of discipline will strengthen us. I'm not convinced that suffering in and of itself creates strength. It's our *response* to the suffering that does that. The discipline of rejoicing in suffering is a response that bears fruit. We can rejoice even in suffering because of the harvest of peace and righteousness we will certainly enjoy when the training is complete.

Right after James gives us reason to rejoice, he reminds us what the result will be: "You know that these troubles test your faith, and this will give you patience" (James 1:3, NCV). We all can use a good dose of patience—and most of us could use it right now! But interestingly enough, the original Greek word means far more than passive endurance. It refers to the kind of perseverance that actively overcomes the trials of life.

A great example of this kind of patience was the brilliant composer Ludwig van Beethoven. When he realized that he would be deaf—a musician's greatest nightmare—he said, "I will take life by the throat." That's the kind of tenacity James is talking about.

Perseverance is one fruit of rejoicing in sufferings. Paul tells us what else God has promised: "We also rejoice in our sufferings, because we know that suffering produces perseverance; perseverance, character; and character, hope. And hope does not disappoint us, because God has poured out his love into our hearts by the Holy Spirit, whom he has given us" (Romans 5:3–5).

God's loving purpose is to conform us to the image of His Son, and Peter reminds us that persevering in trials is how we become more like Him: "In this you greatly rejoice, though now for a little while you may have had to suffer grief in all kinds of trials. These have come so that your faith—of greater worth than gold, which perishes even though refined by fire—may be proved genuine and may result in praise, glory and honor when Jesus Christ is revealed" (1 Peter 1:6–7).

The character produced by rejoicing in hardship is Christlike character—His glory revealed in us—and that character produces hope.

In the New Living Translation, Romans 5:3–5 reads this way:

We can rejoice, too, when we run into problems and trials, for we know that they are good for us—they help us learn to endure. And endurance develops strength of character in us, and character strengthens our *confident expectation* of salvation. And this expectation will not disappoint us. For we know how dearly God loves us, because he has given us the Holy Spirit to fill our hearts with his love. (emphasis added)

Hope is the *confident expectation* that God will use our painful circumstances for good. It's what turns a hardship into "a special goodness in the widest sense." Hope is not a wishful "what if." The hope that emerges from Christlike character is certain and confident—sure that "He who has begun a good work in you will complete it" (Philippians 1:6, NKJV). This kind of hope is generated and confirmed in us by the Holy Spirit, who fills our hearts with God's love. It's what allows us to choose to rejoice amid hardships and to say to God, "I will rejoice in *You!*"

A DECISION THAT DELIVERS

One night when our son Clayton was eight months old, Phil and I returned home from an evening out and were greeted by the babysitter, who had frightening news. When she collapsed the stroller, Clayton had fallen headfirst onto the sidewalk. We were very concerned, and Phil checked Clayton for a concussion. He seemed fine.

Over the next three days, however, Clayton grew increasingly uncomfortable and fussy. Eventually he became listless. We were in and out of doctors' offices and hospital emergency rooms. He didn't have the symptoms of a concussion, so doctors were baffled. I didn't know medicine, but I knew my son—and I knew that something was dreadfully wrong. When Clayton began vomiting, we took him to the doctor's office again.

The doctor did another exam, and this one revealed blood in Clayton's diaper—so much blood that we were whisked away to the hospital where a surgeon waited. Clayton's large intestine was turning itself inside out—a condition called "intussusception"—and the damage was so severe that the surgery took several hours.

Friends quickly arrived to give blood and offer prayers. We were on our knees in that waiting room asking God to help our baby when our surgeon interrupted our prayers with the news that the operation had been successful.

"I know you have prayed to your God," he told us, "because your baby should not have survived. It's a miracle that he didn't have to have a colostomy." It was indeed a miracle, and we knelt in humble adoration of our Great Physician.

When we learned that Clayton had to remain in the hospital for at least a week, Phil and I decided to take turns staying with him. Phil would do the night shift, so I went home alone that night. When I entered the empty apartment, powerful feelings bubbled to the surface. I couldn't help but think about how close we came to never having Clayton there with us again. To drown out the silence and hush the myriad emotions of the day, I sat down at the piano and began to play. And as I did, a song began to form in my heart and move beneath my fingers:

> I will rejoice in You
> God of my salvation
> You always see me through
> And I will rejoice in You!

All that remains of that dark July day in 1990 is a physical scar. Over the years, as Clayton has grown larger, his scar has become smaller. When he got old enough to ask me about it, I told him that it meant "God takes care of us."

Perhaps you too have a scar.

You may have trouble rejoicing in it.

But Nehemiah 8:10 tells us that "the joy of the LORD is our strength," so if you think of your scar as a showcase of

God's power to take care of you, you can rejoice in the Savior who strengthens you. And when you do, God will use your joy to minister to others.

A MOURNING THAT MINISTERS

My friend Joni had been married for five years when her husband learned that he had cancer. This was certainly not what she had envisioned when she and Vance stood at the altar to exchange marriage vows just five years earlier. And it was definitely not what she had anticipated when she held their baby girl in the delivery room two years later. Yet as Vance persevered through hospitalizations and treatments, he and Joni prayed and believed for God's healing, even when the living room furniture was removed and a hospital bed was put in its place.

One afternoon while their three-year-old daughter was visiting a friend, Joni left Vance's bedside to answer the phone. When she returned, she realized that her prayers and belief for healing had been answered. God had lovingly and ultimately healed Vance by gently ushering him into heaven.

I met Joni shortly after Vance died. She was early in the mourning process, and there were days when just taking a shower was a paramount achievement for her. There were days when she would begin a sentence with a laugh and end it with tears. And there were days when she couldn't find any words at all.

The way Joni mourned ministered to me. Her sorrow

was a showcase for the joy of the Lord, which became her strength. As I watched her walk boldly through her heartbreak with the kind of perseverance James talks about, our friendship was forged. The joy of the Lord strengthened her even on the darkest days—and it became contagious.

I remember shopping with Joni a couple of years after Vance died. It was near Memorial Day, and she wanted to buy flowers for his grave. We found ourselves in one of those "super centers"—you know, a place where you can purchase a garden hose, pantyhose, and fresh tomatoes all at once! We began to look through the flower arrangements. Evidently we were a little late, because what was left looked pretty bad.

Joni systematically picked up each arrangement.

"These all look awful," she said.

"This one's ugly."

"This one's wilted."

"This one's turning brown."

Finally, in frustration, she laid the last flowers down and said, "These are so ugly that if I put them on Vance's grave, he'd just die!"

We giggled awkwardly—and then roared with laughter!

Often it's hard to rejoice in our circumstances. The difficulty of change, the sickness of a loved one, the pain of loss—these seem to give us little reason for rejoicing. But if you choose to rejoice anyway, your suffering will strengthen you in your faith walk, your joy will showcase the power of God, and your mourning will minister to others. You have

God's word that "He will give beauty for ashes, joy instead of mourning, praise instead of despair" (Isaiah 61:3, NLT). So if life presents you with a burn, a scar, or wilted grave flowers…rejoice!

> *Rejoice in the Lord always.*
> *I will say it again: Rejoice!*
>
> PHILIPPIANS 4:4

Pure Gold

Sitting with this man of God
Looking at his life
A young man sent to a foreign land
With his children and his wife

For years he was found faithful
And if the truth be told
He came out pure gold

I've seen her age in beauty
I've seen God's truth unfold
For years she served Him fervently
Even when her call felt old

I've seen her in the fire
I've seen her stand so bold
And she came out pure gold

So hang on dear believer
He rewards those who endure
When you feel refining fire
You will know you'll become pure

For there's such a cloud of witnesses
Who applaud you when you hold
You'll come out pure gold

I have searched for inspiration
In the pages of my mind
And it's those who stood adversity
That encouraged me to find
Pure gold

You'll come out pure gold
Stay with the fight
And earn the right
For God's riches to unfold
You'll see many a trial
You'll be tried by the fire
And you'll come out pure gold

WORDS AND MUSIC BY JENNIFER ROTHSCHILD © 1993 ROTHSCHILD MUSIC (ASCAP)

Six

RUN *with* ENDURANCE

⁓

For several summers when I was a teenager, I attended a Christian camp in Black Mountain, North Carolina. One summer early in my blindness, I arrived at camp without my cane. It hadn't yet become an extension of my right arm, and I was still at a point where I didn't want it to be obvious that I couldn't see. So I muddled through without it by just going places I was familiar with.

One night, however, a group of us girls decided to t.p. the car of the cutest guy in camp. The plan was to pull the prank after dark, and there was no way I was going to miss out on the fun. I was as thrilled as the others as we carried out our covert operation. Our egos swelled with pride—until we heard the sound of a car coming toward us.

"It's camp security!" someone cried.

We immediately began to run. As we fled into the darkness, I instinctively grabbed a fellow escapee's arm. In our frenzied flight I lost my grip, lost the group, and lost my footing. I did, however, find a tree.

Smack!

I ended up in a ditch, totally disoriented and pretty sore. One of the girls quickly returned to help me, and we ran for home.

The apostle Paul tells us to "run with endurance the race that is set before us" (Hebrews 12:1, NASB). Believe me, I learned the hard way that we can never run with endurance when we're running where we're not supposed to be. If I'd resisted the temptation of that forbidden flirtation, I would have been safe in camp.

But sometimes we *are* in the right place. We're running the race God has marked out for us, and we're trying to run with endurance. So why is it that we sometimes still threaten to hit the wall?

It's because often there are unanticipated hurdles in our path that we can clear only by stripping away anything that could weigh us down or trip us up as we run. That's why in the same verse, Paul also tells us to "lay aside every encumbrance and the sin which so easily entangles us." Sin will get us off track and leave us disoriented, and before we know it, we can find ourselves in a ditch.

STAY ON TRACK

In 1991, Phil and I moved to Tallahassee, Florida, so he could pursue his Ph.D. This meant that he traded in his job and salary for the financial status of a graduate student. If you're unfamiliar with that status, I can sum it up for you in two words: *no dinero.* No, that isn't Spanish for *no dinner*—although it could have meant that on Phil's wages as a teaching assistant. It means "no money," which was a pretty accurate description of our finances—and the reason we had to call a family budget meeting.

Red pen in hand, Phil prepared to excise the expense of anything not essential to our new lifestyle. One of the first things cut from the list was fabric softener. We figured that as long as the clothes were clean, it really didn't matter if they were stiff or full of static.

I'll admit I was a bit disappointed. Because I can't see, I really don't care if my laundry is stained or discolored after I wash it. I just want it to smell good, and I'd grown accustomed to the fragrance of Bounce on my freshly laundered clothes. But it was a small sacrifice, and I got over my initial disappointment.

Or so I thought.

After a week in our new apartment, I grabbed a basketful of dirty clothes and headed for the laundry room. When I arrived, the room was empty except for me, my dirty laundry…and one big temptation. Someone had left behind an industrial size box of Bounce. It was so huge that even I could see it. It beckoned me. *Come, smell, partake....*

I dropped the basket in front of the washer and reached out to grab the box. *God knows how faithful I've been to keep our new budget!* I thought. *And He's left this here for me!* I was already drafting a letter for financial guru Larry Burkett to read on the air when a voice interrupted my thoughts.

That is not your fabric softener.

I didn't have to look around for the source of the voice— I knew!

You're right, Lord; that's not my fabric softener. I sighed and began to load the washer.

After I shoved in the last dirty dish towel and lowered the lid, I thought, *If this box of Bounce is still here when I come back to fill the dryer, I'll just assume that it was left here for me. After all, my God owns the cattle on a thousand hills. He even owns the hills! Surely He provided this Bounce for me!*

But as I walked back to my apartment, I heard the voice again. *That is not your fabric softener.* I gave a spiritual shrug and (reluctantly) agreed.

While I waited for the wash cycle to finish, I tidied up my kitchen, and as I swept the floor, I began to list my justifications. Finally I announced out loud the top five reasons I should take the fabric softener.

1. I want it!
2. If I take it, no one will ever know.
3. If it wasn't meant to be mine, why was it left there?

4. Blind people need good smelling laundry.
5. The Bounce would be a blessing to me.

(Note: when attempting to justify sin, be sure to use spiritual words like *blessing*.)

I put away the broom and headed back to the "integrity torture chamber." The Bounce was still there, demanding a response. I stared it down as I put the wet, crumpled laundry in the dryer. But before I shut the door, I turned back to that box and lifted the lid. *One sheet,* I told myself, *just one itty-bitty sheet.*

As my guilty fingers clutched it, I once again heard the voice. *That is not your fabric softener.* It was as if I'd been arm wrestling with God and finally my arm went limp.

You're right, Lord. It's not my fabric softener—not even one little sheet of it. I went back to my apartment without the fabric softener, but with a new sense of how sin can sneak in and trip me up.

Now don't miss the point. In the grand scheme of things it doesn't seem that taking a sheet of fabric softener is a big deal. After all, it's not like robbing a bank or stealing someone's husband! But every day we are challenged in the laundry rooms of life with issues of integrity and purity, and private thoughts that aren't submitted to the still, small voice of the Holy Spirit will eventually lead to public failures. We are to resist *all* sin, and Paul reminds us that God never asks us to do something that He doesn't empower us to do:

No temptation has overtaken you but such as is common to man; and God is faithful, who will not allow you to be tempted beyond what you are able, but with the temptation will provide the way of escape also, so that you will be able to endure it. (1 Corinthians 10:13, NASB)

We must learn to confront temptation and sin head-on by obeying God. Otherwise, what may seem to be molehills will become mountains in our path, making it impossible for us to run with endurance.

Running with endurance means not only resisting and repenting of sin, but also giving up things that can hinder our ability to run. Sometimes that means giving up a good thing, for even a good thing can become a weight if isn't the best thing.

SHED SOME WEIGHT

One Sunday morning after I'd had William the guide dog for several months, he and I were sitting attentively in our Bible-study group. Well, actually, I was trying to be attentive to the teacher, but it was awfully hard because William's attention was riveted on a grasshopper that had made its way into our room via an open door. William was determined to catch that critter—even if he had to knock over a stack of Bibles and three Baptists in the process! He slapped his paws forward and jerked his head in pursuit. I, of course, was holding him on a leash and could feel his every move. With each muscle twitch, I pulled the leash a little more firmly.

Well, the tension in the room and the tension in the leash gave all at once as William defied gravity and all seventy pounds of him pounced on the grasshopper. The Bible teacher recoiled as William surged forward. Phil quickly subdued the mischievous mutt, and everyone laughed.

Everyone, but me, that is.

My friend Lori, who was sitting next to me, knew exactly why I wasn't laughing, and she instinctively rose with me. We excused ourselves, leaving William with the class in the hope that he would "get some religion."

In the months after William and I arrived home from the dog school, things hadn't gone as well as I had hoped. One day he bolted up onto the platform at my church while I was singing. And once when we were at the mall, he relieved his bladder right in front of Petite Sophisticates. It was a mess! I didn't even know it was happening until some man graphically described it to me. Then I had to somehow manage to maintain my dignity while I cleaned up the mess. Believe me, at that moment this petite did not look or feel very sophisticated!

Many incidents like these over the previous months had made me feel like giving up trying to use a guide dog, and it all came to a head that Sunday. As soon as Lori and I entered the ladies' room, I burst into tears. "It's just not working," I cried. "This is more of a liability than an asset. I've never wanted to quit so badly before, but—I don't know if I should."

As she almost always does, Lori responded judiciously.

"Jennifer," she said, "if you were deaf, you'd want to wear hearing aids that fit your ears. It would be discreet and practical. I don't think you'd function as well with big ol' Mickey Mouse ears hanging on either side of your head." I giggled with relief at Lori's homespun Southern wisdom. "Giving the guide dog back doesn't mean you're giving up or giving in just because it's hard," she said.

Endurance isn't a virtue if you persevere just to prove you're not a quitter. The point of running with endurance is to run well and finish the race—to do God's will as we follow the course until we reach the finish line. This means that once in a while we have to assess our lives to see if there's anything we need to get rid of. Serious runners in a race don't carry ice chests and portable tape players. They don't carry a change of clothes just in case there's a change in the weather, and they definitely don't have a Happy Meal in hand. Tape players, Happy Meals, and extra clothes are all good things, but none of them are the best things to carry while running a race.

A guide dog is a good thing. I could trust William to get me safely where I wanted to go. But for me he wasn't the best thing, because instead of enhancing my ability to run, he hindered it. Any good thing can weigh us down if we substitute it for what is really best.

In order to run well, we must listen to God. He has great plans for us and knows the best way for us to succeed. "'For I know the plans that I have for you,' declares the LORD, 'plans for welfare and not for calamity to give you a future and a hope'" (Jeremiah 29:11, NASB). God is our Coach. He's run this way before, and He can guide us through the choices and help us over the hurdles.

RUN TO GOD

In the Gospels we see many needy people running to Jesus. Mark tells us about a rich young man who had a need and knew that Jesus could tell him how to meet it.

"As Jesus started on his way," Mark writes, "a man ran up to him and fell on his knees before him. 'Good teacher,' he asked, 'what must I do to inherit eternal life?'" (Mark 10:17). When Jesus answered by reminding him of the commandments that any upstanding Jewish citizen would obey, the man said, "Teacher…all these I have kept since I was a boy" (v. 20). Mark says that when the rich young man said this, "Jesus looked at him and loved him" (v. 21).

The man had led a decent, respectable life. But inheriting eternal life involves much more than respectability; it requires complete commitment to Christ. And because Jesus loved the man, He told him what he really needed.

"One thing you lack," He said. "Go, sell everything you have and give to the poor, and you will have treasure in heaven. Then come, follow me." Mark says that "at this the man's face fell. He went away sad, because he had great wealth" (vv. 20–22). This was not what the rich man had expected to hear, and he was not willing to strip down for the race.

Just like the rich man, we often run to Jesus and fall down before Him because we have needs that only He can meet. And Jesus looks at us and loves us. We feel His penetrating gaze and His enveloping love. But then we hear His words, and sometimes our faces fall and we go away sad because He doesn't tell us what we want to hear. What He tells us to do seems like too great a sacrifice.

But whatever that sacrifice might be, it's small compared to the prize we receive in His presence. So don't run to Him with preconceived notions or an agenda.

Just run to Him to be with Him.

Run to Him with abandon.

Fall before Him, and cling to Him alone.

He knows what you truly need, and you'll never be disappointed. In fact, you will be amazed and overwhelmed, just like the folks in Mark 9:15: "As soon as all the people saw Jesus, they were overwhelmed with wonder and ran to greet him." They saw something in Jesus that the rich man missed—something that was worth everything. When was the last time you caught a true glimpse of Jesus? If you truly see Him, you too will be overwhelmed with wonder, and you will run to Him.

Always remember that after you've run for a while, the race begins to feel long. As you pound the pavement, winded and weary, you can easily get discouraged and feel like dropping out before you reach the finish line. Charles Spurgeon, the great preacher, felt that way so often that he tried to resign thirty-two times! To keep in the race, I bet he had to remind himself of Hebrews 10:36: "Patient endurance is what you need now, so you will continue to do God's will. Then you will receive all that he has promised" (NLT).

Staying in the race takes something more substantial than not wanting to quit. It takes something more important than wishing our needs were met. It even takes something more gratifying than yearning to reach the goal. It takes a deep desire for God. David knew what it was to desire God and to run to Him. "My soul followeth hard after thee," he said (Psalm 63:8, KJV). Another psalmist described his longing for God this way: "As the deer pants for the water brooks, so pants my soul for You, O God" (Psalm 42:1, NKJV).

Do you remember what it felt like in P.E. class when you had to run laps around the perimeter of the basketball courts? I do! I know what it felt like to pant after running so hard. But what I really want to know is what it feels like for my soul to pant after God with the kind of intensity the psalmist describes. When we run to Him with that level of desire, we'll be breathless, and He will become the air we breathe.

Do you run after God with that intensity? Does your soul follow hard after God? Running after God will always be strengthening and motivating. When our souls follow hard after Him, He upholds us with His right hand (Psalm 63:8). I believe that running with endurance is easy when we run to God out of complete desire to know Him and to be with Him.

When I was eight years old, I ran to Jesus in my heart, and He saw me and loved me. He saw my greatest need, and He saved me. Now the path to Him is familiar and well-worn. I run to Him on it daily because I desire to know Him. Every day we have the opportunity to run with urgent desire to show Him that we love Him and want to serve Him. And even though we don't deserve it, when God sees us quicken our pace toward Him, He Himself runs to meet us.

GO FOR THE GOLD

During the 1992 Olympics in Barcelona, a young runner from Great Britain crouched in the block at the starting line, ready for the run of his life. Derek Redmond's lifelong dream was to win a gold medal in the four-hundred-meter run, and now he had made it to the semifinal heat. The gun sounded and Derek ran with all his might. He was running well...until a pulled hamstring sent him sprawling facedown on the track.

Determined to finish the race, Derek somehow got to his feet and began to hop toward the finish line. As he struggled, an older man made his way down from the stands. Showing the same kind of determination as the injured runner, he made his way through the crowds, pushing aside security guards. When he reached Derek, a great crowd of spectators watched Jim Redmond throw his large arms around his son. Jim stayed in his son's lane, supporting Derek the entire time, and when they crossed the finish line together, the onlookers were on their feet, weeping and cheering.

Derek Redmond didn't win the gold medal that day, but he walked away from the race knowing that he had a father who loved him too much to stay in the stands watching him suffer.

That's the kind of Father we have.

You know that, don't you?

He's a Father who loves us too much to stand back and watch us struggle and suffer. He comes down from the stands and joins us as we run.[1]

In Luke 15, Jesus draws a word picture of how God responds to us when we come to Him. He tells a story of a father with two sons. The younger of the two insisted that his father give him his inheritance early. Then he left home and squandered the money on reckless living. When the money ran out, so did his dignity, and he stooped to feeding swine so he wouldn't starve.

At last the son resolved to return home. "So he got up and went to his father," Luke tells us. "But while he was still

a long way off, his father saw him and was filled with compassion for him; he ran to his son, threw his arms around
him and kissed him" (Luke 15:20).

When our Father sees us making strides toward home,
He runs to meet us.

If the race seems too long and you begin to lose heart,
run to God, and He will run to you. "Come near to God,"
writes James, "and he will come near to you" (James 4:8).
He will strengthen you and help you finish the race.

In Hebrews 12:1, Paul says that you are surrounded by a
great cloud of witnesses, the great heroes of the faith who
have run that way before you. They are cheering you on,
because they know that the reward of running with
endurance is sure. When you cross that finish line, you'll not
only get the prize—you'll come out pure gold.

I guide you in the way of wisdom and
lead you along straight paths.
When you walk, your steps will not be hampered;
when you run, you will not stumble.

PROVERBS 4:11–12

To Be like You

Sometimes I feel just like a stranger
The things I think put me in danger
And I want so much to be
Constrained by purity
Oh, Lord, will I ever be like You?

Inside my mind there is an image
Of what the world expects to see
But regardless of my call
I still so often fall
Oh, Lord, will I ever be like You?

To be like You
In the quiet of my heart
To be like You
In the deepest private part
To struggle with my humanity
Yet to cling to purity
Is to be, to be like You

Sometimes I feel weakness defines me
Yet still I pray weakness refines me
But no matter what the case
I am desperate for Your grace
Oh, Lord, will I ever be like You?

To be like You
In the quiet of my heart
To be like You
In the deepest private part
To struggle with my humanity
Yet to cling to purity
Is to be, to be like You

WORDS AND MUSIC BY JENNIFER ROTHSCHILD © 1993 ROTHSCHILD MUSIC (ASCAP)

Seven

FALL *Down...* GET UP

M y shining moment as a communication major at Palm Beach Atlantic College occurred in Professor McGee's "Fundamentals of Acting" class in the fall of my junior year. By then I had already muddled through the basics of blocking, character development, and improvisation, and there was one thing I knew for sure—Katharine Hepburn I was not!

But one day Professor McGee announced that he was going to teach us the art of skillful falling, and suddenly I felt confident. *Yes!* I thought. *Finally, something I'm good at!* When you're blind, falling comes with the territory, and by then I'd had lots of experience at it.

I'd fallen up stairs.

I'd fallen into holes.

I'd fallen down hills.

I'd fallen just about everywhere.

Now I was ready to show my stuff!

After Professor McGee taught us to fall convincingly but safely, he set the scene for us. We were a group of towns-people all busily doing our jobs. Unbeknownst to us, there was a murderer among us, and when he caught our eye, he would wink, meaning *Bang! You're dead!* Then we were to fall to our demise as we'd been taught. Because I couldn't see, Professor McGee said that instead of winking, the murderer would tap my back.

The professor gave each of us a prop to use in our improvisation. Mine was a broom, so when he yelled "Action," I began to sweep. All around me my classmates busied themselves with their tasks. Suddenly one of them fell. Within minutes, another one went down. Professor McGee threaded his way through our band of thespians, monitoring falls and carefully stepping over fallen students.

I heard a young man fall to my right and felt his feather duster land on my foot. Then I heard Professor McGee moving toward me, and soon I felt the pat of death. The moment to display my falling prowess was at hand, and as luck would have it, the professor was right in front of me. He would have a front-row view of my acting talent. Without hesitation, I folded my knees and collapsed my shoulders—and down I went, all in one relaxed, fluid, flawless fall.

But Professor McGee didn't get to witness my glorious moment. Yes, he was standing right in front of me—but not for long. When I let go of the broom, it landed on his...I mean between his...well, let's just say he doubled over in pain and then staggered off to his office trying to catch his breath.

While my classmates convulsed in laughter, I lay there for a moment not quite sure what had happened. I only knew that right after class I was going to the registrar's office to change my major to psychology. Oh, it was so embarrassing!

When we fall in our faith walk, we can also end up surprised, confused, and embarrassed. Falling isn't anything we plan. It just happens. Something trips us up, and down we go. And sadly, falling is not a one-time deal. We're all going to encounter lots of spiritual stumbling blocks. Some of these may just cause us to stagger, but others might result in a nose-first face plant on the ground. When that happens, it hurts. And unfortunately, our fall can hurt others, too. (Just ask Mr. McGee!)

To avoid falling, we need to learn more about why it happens. Since I'm a card-carrying frequent faller (in the physical sense), I've learned a bit about it. Perhaps what I've learned can help you.

What Makes Us Fall?

It was the end of spring semester, time to say good-bye to my college buddies for the summer. Soon my dad would arrive to transport me home, so I began packing all my worldly goods. I placed my B. J. Thomas and Amy Grant cassettes neatly in boxes. I carefully rolled up my rainbow posters and placed them in cylinders. I meticulously arranged my twenty-two pairs of shoes in their individual boxes and stacked them up. (Oh, was I prissy)! At last everything was ready for Dad and the U-Haul.

When Dad arrived, he surveyed my stuff and then issued marching orders. He told me which items to take and in what order. We must have made thirty treks up and down those familiar dormitory stairs. Finally only my hanging clothes were left. They were my passion—my very identity!—and with so much at stake, I took charge. I told Dad which clothes to take first and how he should carry them.

I saved the best for last—my nicest suits, dresses, and pantsuits. I was certain that I was the only one who could carry them correctly and put them in just the right place. I folded the generous stack over my arm and headed down the stairs.

"Wait, I'll come get those," my dad called out.

"Oh no, Dad, I'm fine," I replied. Confidently, I continued speeding downward.

"Be careful," he called again. "You're going too fast."

"Really, Dad. I've got them. I'm fine." And I thought I was! I practically pranced down those stairs with my treasures. I was in charge, in a hurry, and invincible. I was also just three steps from the bottom when I lost my footing and began to tumble.

In the few seconds it took to complete my descent, all I could think about were my beloved clothes. Soaring through the air, I imagined the damage about to be inflicted on my wardrobe, and instead of dropping the clothes so I would have a soft landing field, I held them high to keep them out of harm's way. The Olympic runner falling across the finish line with torch held high—that was me! (Liz Claiborne should have personally thanked me for my selflessness.)

Mentally and physically unbalanced, I collapsed under the weight of freshly dry-cleaned rayon. The real casualty was a broken ankle. But I think what hurt most was my shattered pride. I'd always heard that "pride goes before a fall," but before that day, I had assumed that it was just a figurative expression.

When I thought back on that incident, I could see a number of reasons why I fell, and it occurred to me that they are the very things that can cause us to fall in our spiritual walk as well. Learning to recognize these stumbling blocks can help keep us upright.

Stumbling Block #1: Pride

I did not take the stairs seriously enough, and I took myself much too seriously. Sometimes when we're familiar with life's routine, we don't consider the potential pitfalls in our path. Pride can seep in and convince us that we are in charge, sufficient, and independent. Proverbs 18:12 reminds us that "before his downfall a man's heart is proud, but humility comes before honor." That also goes for the heart of a female obsessed with fashion! Clothing ourselves in humility protects us from falling, and a little humility is far less painful than a lot of humiliation.

Are you prancing with pride, or are you walking humbly with your God?

Stumbling Block #2: Priorities

I protected the wrong thing. Yes, my life's savings were tied up in that mangled mess of material that landed on top of me at the bottom of the stairs. But was it really worth a broken ankle? I suspect that if my priority had been safety instead of vanity, the result of the fall would have been different, or perhaps I wouldn't have fallen at all. "Be careful how you walk," the apostle Paul warns us, "not as unwise men but as wise" (Ephesians 5:15, NASB). We'll be secure in our spiritual walk when we recognize what is *truly* important and allow Him to direct us.

Do the right priorities direct your steps, or do misplaced ones cause you to stumble?

Stumbling Block #3: Preoccupation

I was in a hurry. In my rush to complete my task, I failed to follow the disciplines that allow me to navigate safely, like counting the stairs and holding on to the rails. Sometimes schedules and the pressing demands of life set us up for a fall. Being busy, even with good things, can distract us from the best.

When God commands us to "be still" (Psalm 46:10), it's so we'll take time to learn about Him. When we do this, the frenzied pace of life is less likely to lead to a fall. If we learn to schedule stillness into our lives, we'll find rest in the rat race as we lean into Him.

Is your discipline in your calendar, or in your heart?

Stumbling Block #4: Pressure

I carried too much stuff. I'd obviously forgotten how the limitations of my blindness affected my ability to walk with an unusually heavy load. It's easier to keep our balance when we monitor the weight of our cargo.

We all need to measure how much we can carry in view of our life situations. Stress inevitably depletes us and leaves us vulnerable to a fall, while keeping a sense of balance not only reduces our chance of falling, but also speeds us on our way. The psalmist said, "I run in the path of your commands, for you have set my heart free"(Psalm 119:32). When we are unencumbered by the stresses of life, we too are free to run.

Are you weighed down with the load you carry, or is liberty your lifestyle?

Once we recognize and learn to avoid these stumbling blocks, it's easier to keep from falling. But unexpected potholes in life can sometimes still trip us up, so it's important to learn how to get back up again when we falter. Why do some people quickly recover from their falls and move on, while others remain prostrate and immobilized after hitting a bump in the road of life?

I'm glad you asked.

Understanding how to get up is as important as learning why we fall. The two go together.

How Can We Get Up?

If the bad news is that sin can trip us up, the good news is that we can get up again. Proverbs 24:16 tells us that "though a righteous man falls seven times, he rises again." When I let pride take over, I stumbled and fell. But I learned from that fall. I was able to look back on it, see what caused the tumble, and ask God to help me avoid it in the future. Once I'd repented, I was able to move forward with renewed confidence.

I'm reminded of a couple of familiar people in the Bible, both of them kings—David and Saul. Here's the JAV version (that's Jennifer's Abridged Version) of their stories.

King Saul failed to destroy the Amalekites as God had commanded. Then, when the prophet Samuel confronted him, he was unwilling to admit his sin and repent of it. Instead, he made excuses and placed blame on others. God was so grieved by his willful disobedience that He withdrew His blessing from Saul's reign. In other words, Saul's sin caused him to fall, but his refusal to acknowledge it and repent kept him lying flat on the ground.

Read the rest of Saul's story in 1 Samuel 15, and then compare it to the story of David in 2 Samuel 11. King David not only failed to lead his people in battle as God had commanded, but he compounded that sin by committing adultery with the wife of Uriah, one of his officers. If that wasn't bad enough, he then attempted to cover up his sin by having Uriah killed.

Unlike Saul, however, David's sin broke his heart. His prayer of repentance clearly reveals why he recovered from his fall: "I know my transgressions, and my sin is always before me. Against you, you only, have I sinned" (Psalm 51:3–4). David bounced back after his fall because he humbled himself and repented.

Both Saul and David had pretty nasty falls, but it was their heart's response to the sin that determined whether they would get up. The Bible tells us that David was a man after God's own heart (1 Samuel 13:14). If a man like David felt it necessary to ask God to create in him a pure heart, how much more do we need to ask for the same thing? We need cleansed hearts to keep us choosing the right path. Our feet will tread the paths our hearts pursue.

WHERE ARE WE WALKING?

If you're walking through a flowerbed and you fall, you can pretty much assume that you'll end up smelling like a rose. But if you're strolling through the city dump and you trip over an old tire, all the Tide in the supermarket won't be able to remove the stench.

When I was in the ninth grade, my family visited my grandparents. My granddaddy had several stout hunting dogs. While my brothers played, I tiptoed over to the dog pen. I opened the gate and, once inside, closed it quickly behind me. Then the party began. Were those dogs happy to see me! It was canine chaos. Vying for my attention, those big hounds began to jump up on me to lick my face, and almost immediately, they knocked me to the ground. As I lay there, I noticed a peculiar aroma filling the air. Actually, it would have been hard not to notice, since I was lying in its source. The happy dogs were prancing all over me, leaving behind their smelly reminder that I had fallen in the *wrong* place.

As I discovered in the dog pen, we need to be careful where we walk. We must choose our paths wisely on our faith walk as well. Sometimes a path may appear harmless, but if you stumble there, you might end up in quicksand. "There is a way that seems right to a man," says Proverbs 14:12, "but in the end it leads to death."

I have a friend who used to enjoy Internet chat rooms. They seemed innocent enough—until she become emotionally involved with a fellow chatter and found herself drowning in the quicksand of adultery.

I'm not saying that we can't chat on the Internet; we just must be mindful of our individual weaknesses. A path that is harmless for one may be deadly for another. You can't become a chocoholic if you never plant a Hershey's kiss on your lips, and it's impossible to get into credit card debt if you don't own those persuasive little pieces of plastic.

"In the way of righteousness there is life; along that path is immortality," says Proverbs 12:28. Where do you walk? Does each step lead you toward life, or does it lead you toward death? If you stumble there, will you fall on the Rock, or will you end up sinking like one? We need to choose wisely where we walk.

Who Is Walking with Us?

Okay, by now it's obvious: I'm into falling! Although most of my falls haven't been intentional, there have been times when I have chosen to fall.

One time was when Philip and I had been married for about six years. We were on a vacation in Pigeon Forge, Tennessee, where a seven-story bungee-jumping platform caught my husband's eye. This triggered him to challenge me. I believe his exact words were: "You would *never* bungee jump!"

"Would so," I shot back.

"Would not!"

"Would so!"

"Would not." Then we began to exchange chicken sounds—you know: *pok, pok, pok!*

We may have been married for six years, but we were acting like six-year-olds. As a result of our childish banter, I ended up buckled in a safety harness and tied to a bungee cord. There I was—seven stories above common sense! And when the platform attendant said "Jump," I did! At first the falling was euphoric. I felt free, yet secure; weightless, yet strangely grounded. I actually liked it until the bungee stretched to its full extension and jerked me back into the inescapable reality that I had just broken the law of gravity and was now falling *up.*

In many ways life is like bungee jumping. We fall down. We get up. What makes the difference is what we are tied to. The reason I felt secure in my seven-story fall was that I knew I was tied to something immovable. As believers, our security is found in the law of spiritual gravity. Never heard of spiritual gravity? That's okay, neither had Isaac Newton, but boy, did he need it. We all do.

When Christ found us, we had already fallen, just as if we had jumped off a seven-story platform—tied to nothing. We were doomed, with no hope of recovery. Then His forgiveness became our bungee cord. When He redeemed us, He fastened us to Himself, wrapping us safely in the unbreakable cords of His great salvation. As the writer of Hebrews tells us, "We have this hope as an anchor for the soul, firm and secure" (Hebrews 6:19).

Once we are fastened to Christ, our heavenly Father lovingly guides us as we learn to walk with Him. Jude assures us that He is a reliable companion, one we can hang on to as we travel life's journey: "To him who is able to keep you from falling and to present you before His glorious presence without fault and with great joy" (Jude 1:24).

My decision to bungee jump wasn't the only time I've chosen to fall. In fact, I deliberately fall on a regular basis. Let me explain.

I know that it's hard for fully sighted people to imagine what it must be like to walk in the dark every day. And I know that they wonder how a blind person can carry out daily routines, handle a career, or raise kids. I know, because I was once fully sighted. I understand both worlds.

I admit that some days the weight of blindness falls heavy upon me. Sometimes even a simple thing like wearing matching socks can seem like a monumental challenge. *How will I get to the grocery store?* I ask myself. *Who will read my mail to me and clip the baby's fingernails?* When those times come, blindness becomes an uninvited guest that stifles my dreams by turning ordinary routines into such extraordinary tasks that they leave me worn out and discouraged. On those mornings, when the list of questions is longer than the list of answers, my fatigue seems more powerful than my faith, and not even sheer grit seems enough to propel me out of bed to face the day.

So guess what I do?

Before I get up, I fall down.

Yes, you read that right: Before I get up, I fall down! The *ultimate* fall is the one that happens in my heart when, with complete abandon, I yield my entire self and fall before my Father. He finds me there in my weakness and lovingly lifts me, reminding me of what the prophet Isaiah wrote:

> "How can you say the LORD does not see your troubles?… Don't you know that the LORD is the everlasting God, the Creator of all the earth? He never grows faint or weary.… He gives power to those who are tired and worn out; he offers strength to the weak." (Isaiah 40: 27–29, NLT)

That's the really wonderful thing I've learned about falling: On days when I can't rise, He *carries* me. God's great love for us is there to sustain us even when we can't get up after we fall. If you make sure that your first fall every morning is the one in which you surrender yourself completely to Him, you will find strength for the journey.

> *Cast your cares on the LORD and he will sustain you;*
> *he will never let the righteous fall.*
>
> PSALM 55:22

Unfailing Love

I will trust in Your unfailing love
My heart rejoices in Your salvation
I will sing unto the Lord
For He has been good to me

Your goodness like the rainfall
Washes over me
I dance beneath the starlight
As You're dancing over me
Joy is now my heartbeat
Freedom is my song
So I soar on the wings of Your love

I will trust in Your unfailing love
My heart rejoices in Your salvation
I will sing unto the Lord
For He has been good to me

WORDS AND MUSIC BY JENNIFER ROTHSCHILD © 1997 ROTHSCHILD MUSIC

Eight

DANCE *the* NIGHT AWAY

.

I f Webster were to allow me to make one spelling change in the English language, it would be this: I would change the third *e* in *independence* to *a*, and then the word would read *independance*. I like it so much better that way, because when the last five letters spell *dance*, the word makes me think of a life that is joyful and free. But then two other words would also end in *dance: dependance* and *interdependance*.

See, it's all a dance!

It's just a matter of listening to the music and learning how to respond.

Phil and I celebrated our tenth anniversary aboard a cruise ship. After our trip through the dessert line at the first midnight buffet, we realized that we were going to have to do something to burn all those extra calories. So I donned sequins, and off we went to the dance floor. It didn't take us long to realize that we needed lessons, and along with several other couples, we met with the dance instructor in the ball-room. *This will be fun,* I thought. Even though Phil and I had never danced before, I was determined to take the risk and not be self-conscious.

The music began, the instructor described and demonstrated each step we were to take, and Phil clumsily imitated her. I held on to him and tried to match his movements.

There we were: Phil, uncoordinated. Me, blind. We stepped on each other's feet and bumped into other dancers—and we weren't even doing the two-step or the bump. We were quite a spectacle!

After a while, we relaxed and began to follow the rhythm of the music. Soon we were actually dancing. It would have been less embarrassing for me and much safer for the other dancers if I'd never fox-trotted onto the scene, but oh, what I would have missed! It was worth risking my composure and feeling clumsy, because dancing made me feel surprisingly free. Yes, I depended on Phil for my every move. But we knew each other so well that when we connected in the movements of the dance, it felt fabulous!

There's a lot to be said for depending on others and becoming interdependent. But there are some dance lessons I've had to learn the hard way.

Celebrating In-Dependence Day

Like any other eighteen-year-old, I saw going away to college as a major step on my road to independence—to making my way in the world just as others did. As a freshman at Palm Beach Atlantic College, my greatest desire was to blend in. I didn't want to be known as "the new blind girl." I just wanted to be known as the new girl.

So I loved the fact that, as often as not, it wasn't obvious that I couldn't see. It was as if I could hide the painful reality of my blindness behind a facade that made me feel "normal."

One afternoon near the end of freshman orientation, after being tossed from meeting to meeting all day, I felt educated, irritated, placated...and dilapidated! Worn out, I decided to spend a few moments alone in the chapel before the final orientation meeting.

The campus was located on the intercoastal waterway in West Palm Beach, and the chapel was in the waterside amphitheater. To get to it, I had to cross Flagler Drive, a busy four-lane thoroughfare. By then I was accustomed to listening for the ebb and flow of traffic, so I stood confidently on the edge of the curb, ready to cross. But I didn't extend my cane, because I really didn't want the drivers of the passing cars to know I was blind. I could just imagine what they would think: *What is she doing? How dangerous!*

So I waited until I heard a lull in the traffic, took a deep breath, prayed...and *ran!* One lane, two lanes.... *Whew!*

What I didn't know was that the cars in the third and fourth lanes were going the opposite direction. I was terrified. I couldn't tell what was coming from where. I almost ran into a car, and the driver slowed just long enough to yell some choice locker-room words at me. I was humiliated, but I made it safely across. I'm sure my secret service angels filed an official complaint: *You didn't tell us we'd signed up for hazardous duty!*

I staggered into the amphitheater and collapsed into a seat. No one else was there. Not even my common sense had joined me—I'd left that on the other side of Flagler Drive. As my adrenaline rush faded and I began to think about what I'd done, a wave of nausea swept over me. *What did I think I was doing? How dangerous! I'll never do that again, God, I promise!* And boy, did I mean it! That close call squelched my desire to look normal and be independent.

Sitting there all alone in the Chapel by the Lake, I realized that independence is not all it's cracked up to be. In our search for it, we often end up in isolation. The same is true when we act independently of God. But fortunately, the unintended consequences of our self-reliance can often reveal our need for a helper, someone to rescue us—a Savior.

After I repented and started to regroup, I suddenly realized that I had no way to get back to campus. My meeting was in twenty minutes, and I was stuck. Now I knew I'd really blown it. *Will I even make it back before curfew?* I wondered. Hoping that a fellow student would walk by, I decided to stay put. I continued to pray as I listened for pedestrians.

Five minutes passed. Silence.

Ten minutes. Silence.

Far from blending in, I was totally alone, and I imagined college staffers out looking for the new blind girl.

A deep voice behind me interrupted my thoughts: "Miss, do you need help?"

I spun around. *Is it that obvious?* I asked myself.

It was a police officer. "Well…actually…," I stammered. Then, swallowing my pride, I told him all about my mortifying misadventure. When I finished, the policeman was really excited.

Excited?

Well, as it turned out, he had a story to tell, too—and it was even better than mine! He told me that he was scheduled to work security for the six o'clock service at the chapel and that he'd been home watching a football game when suddenly he became very distracted and felt an urgency to leave for work— more than an hour early. He told me he was a Christian and said he knew that God had been nudging him to go. Now he knew why, and he could hardly contain his excitement.

I was stunned. A stubborn, self-absorbed eighteen-year-old girl sat by the water and prayed. A kind and merciful Father answered. An obedient and loving policeman came to my rescue.

I wish I knew that officer's name. But I do know his

heavenly Father's name. It's Jehovah-Jireh, the God on whom I depend. That day in the chapel was my in-dependence day—the day when the fact that I had lost my independence was seared upon my heart. But it also catapulted me into the arms of God, changing my longing for independence into a desire to be a dependent daughter.

"My God will meet all your needs according to his glorious riches in Christ Jesus," Paul assures us in Philippians 4:19. Because the Lord is who He says He is and does what He says He will do, I know that I can depend on Him to meet *all* my needs—including my need to feel normal and to blend in.

RISKING WHAT YOU CAN'T LOSE

We can depend fully on the name of the Lord because His name bears His character. But sometimes we are only mildly acquainted with His name—we *know of* Him. God, on the other hand, is intimately acquainted with us—He *knows* us. The psalmist reminds us of that:

> O LORD, you have searched me and you know me.
> You know when I sit and when I rise;
> you perceive my thoughts from afar.
> You discern my going out and my lying down;
> you are familiar with all my ways.
> Before a word is on my tongue you know it completely, O LORD. (Psalm 139:1–4)

One of our most basic needs is to be known. Yet human companionship cannot provide the kind of complete knowing that our soul craves. God alone can do that because, as our Creator and our constant companion, He knows us completely. If we're truly honest, we have to admit that our desire to be known by Him is far greater than our desire to be independent.

Even though I have sometimes ended up isolating myself by choosing to be independent, I have more often felt isolated because independence has chosen me. Blindness may keep me in a state of physical dependence, but I feel the sting of independence most in the spiritual realm. Why? Because I have an overwhelming sense that blindness is a burden not to be shared.

Part of the isolation is a natural result of the fact that for most people blindness is an enigma, a mystery comprehensible on a cognitive level but baffling on an intuitive level. I find that pragmatists tend to casually dismiss it, while the tenderhearted are apt to enter into it with a degree of sympathy that prohibits real connection. Some even romanticize it, marveling at how "perceptive" I must be or how acute my other senses are. People like these think that every blind person longs to feel other people's faces.

Blindness, however, is just one of many things that can create islands within us. We all find ourselves in situations that make us feel isolated. Deep down they create a degree of separation from others because we feel that *no one else can truly understand our circumstances.*

As a result, a feeling of loneliness descends.

It's not an emotional loneliness produced by human feelings and urges, but a sort of soul-loneliness that makes me cry out to be connected by the cords of empathy to Someone who understands without words or explanation.

Sometimes I think that is why I can see God so clearly. Jesus is never fascinated by what I see or don't see. He doesn't marvel from a distance at how I've compensated.

He just knows.

He knows utterly. He knows intimately. To be understood by Him like that is to rest and revel in a place that never needs description. To wander endlessly through His secret place is a sort of freedom that I will never know in the physical realm.

If the isolation that accompanies blindness compels me to a deeper connection with God, I am the richer. All of us need to treasure anything within us that makes us feel just a little detached from the greater arena of human experience, for it may be the one thing that God mercifully gives us to tie us to Himself and fill our need to be known by Him.

A kind of unsought independence, soul-loneliness can teach us that we can depend fully upon the One who knows us so intimately. It should not only make us want to know God even as we are known by Him, but also compel us to risk becoming interdependent by allowing others to know us.

That's the life God designed us for. And since God

already knows us fully and we're eternally secure in Him, we're just risking something we can't lose anyway.

During college orientation, I'd learned that dependence isn't really so bad. A little later on in my freshman year, I learned that we would all be richer if we risked being interdependent. Early that fall, I called my mom with two important pieces of news.

"Mom," I announced excitedly, "I went out with this guy named Curtiss. And he wears an earring!"

I heard a gulp and then a faint sigh. I could tell that Mom was just as excited as I was—an earring, no less! His name wasn't even important; his earring was what mattered.

"And," I continued, "I got to drive Allison's car this morning!"

"You...*what!*" Mom's voice was no longer faint.

"It's true, Mom! We all piled in and went to the empty parking lot of a bank. It was so much fun!"

I wish I could remember my mom's exact words because I'll probably need a similar phrase to use on my kids when they do something foolish. However, I distinctly remember that she was not happy! The good thing was that after I told her about driving the car, dating the guy with an earring seemed completely harmless.

Well, I never did either again, but I did learn an interesting lesson from driving Allison's car. It was just another step in my dance lessons: Dependence is a good thing...and interdependence is even better!

Because Allison could see, I was totally dependent on her to tell me when to turn, when to brake, and how fast to go. And what did my dependence get me? An experience of a lifetime! It was fun—a kind of freedom I hadn't tasted yet—and I loved it! In the same way, we must depend fully on God for our direction in life. When we are willing to do what He tells us to do, we can park our pride at the curb, jump in for the ride of a lifetime, and find a fabulous freedom.

Yes, I had to depend on Allison to tell me how to drive, but she also had to depend on me to do what she said. Life is like that little car crammed with college students. We're all on the journey together, and our lives are filled with people who need us to be dependable. Our relationship with God inevitably affects our relationships with others, and they will find us fully reliable only when we depend fully on Him.

Of course, we all have times when we *aren't* completely reliable. When we don't depend on God for direction, we can fail others and ourselves. But no matter what is going on around us, when we've traded our independence for the freedom of fully depending on God and the fullness of depending on each other, we're ready to dance. We just have to listen for the music!

LISTENING FOR THE MUSIC

In 1996 we moved to Oklahoma. We had been there only a few weeks when the local TV station was all aflutter with warnings: The first tornado of the season was on its way. Our only TV was downstairs in the living room, so I trudged down the stairs, pillow and blanket in hand. I was going to watch the weather till the storm passed. By the time I settled in on the couch, the winds were howling, and the windows in our old town house were rattling with every gust. Just as the meteorologist had predicted, hail and lightning accompanied the wind, and the rain came in monsoonlike swells. It was enough to scare even this Florida girl!

As I cowered beneath the blanket, I began to notice another sound—one that Channel 9 news hadn't predicted. Between wind gusts and lightning crashes, I heard birds chirping. They sounded like newly hatched babies. Evidently, mama bird thought our chimney made a good home for her new arrivals. It was entertaining at first, but it quickly became annoying when Mama joined the chorus.

Mama bird was a full-throated whistler—and boy, was she loud! The soundtrack that evening was a dissonant mix of hail, thunder, wind, chirping, and whistling. Those birds never quit. Between swells, the storm grew silent, but not once did those birds stop singing.

Why aren't they scared? Don't they know there's a storm outside? This is not the time to sing!

But as the storm died down and I began to feel sleepy, it dawned on me. Those birds knew there was a storm, but they sang because they were birds. They responded to the life that was inside them, not the storm that was outside them.

Sometimes storms surround us, and the discordant sounds of our circumstances are so loud that they drown out the music. But deep inside us is a song that can rise from God's presence in our life. Even when the storm rages, our response can echo the melody of freedom within us.

So how can you dance when your independence has left you feeling lonely and isolated? How can you dance when you feel stuck in dependence? How can you dance when interdependence fails you and you find yourself in painful circumstances? Well, I figure we can all take dance lessons from Peter at this point.

You remember Peter. Jesus called him "the rock." Although that doesn't sound as though he was much of a dancer, I think the old fisherman could teach us all how to dance, because in the book of Matthew we see Peter learning to depend fully on the Lord of the dance.

Peter and the other disciples found themselves in the midst of a storm. The wind raged, tossing their boat and testing their courage. Suddenly, they saw someone walking on the surface of the water. After Jesus identified Himself, Peter immediately positioned himself for the dance.

"Lord, if it's you," he said, "tell me to come to you on the water."

"Come," Jesus said.

Jesus invites us to participate in the dance, too. No matter what storm rages around us, He beckons each one of us, just as He did Peter, to come, take a risk, and depend fully on Him.

You know the story. Peter stepped out of that boat into a perilous place that revealed his absolute need for God. Once there, he suddenly realized how hard it really is to dance. Especially over the waves. The Bible tells us that when he saw the raging wind, he became afraid and began to sink. Peter saw the storm raging because he took his eyes off the Lord of the dance. And when he did, the din of the chaos surrounding him drowned out the sound of the Lord's call to freedom.

Peter would have failed dance lessons at this point. He was ready to sink from the weight of his faithlessness. But he cried out three words—the same three words that will keep all of us in step with the rhythm of grace—*"Lord, save me!"* And immediately Jesus reached out and caught him (Matthew 14:28–31).

Sometimes our utter dependence makes us stumble awkwardly toward the arms of God. Sometimes we totter precariously as we learn to strike just the right balance in our interdependent relationships. God knows we are all weak and wobbly dancers, and He is always ready to extend His arm and reach out and catch us.

Lord, save me are my three favorite words in the book of Matthew. I spoke them as a frightened college student stranded at Chapel by the Lake. I whisper them quietly to my heavenly Father today as a wife and mother learning to walk by faith. They are the three most powerful words any of us can speak when we're learning how to dance, for they invite the Lord of the dance to teach us the real freedom that comes from full dependence on Him.

Don't wait for the storm to pass before you sing.

Don't wait for just the right situation in life before you let your spirit cut loose and dance.

You can dance in the dark or when the storm rages. Lean fully on the Lord of the dance. Listen closely, and you'll hear His music in your spirit. Rely on Him for your every step, and you'll experience the joy and freedom of dependence.

You turned my wailing into dancing;
you removed my sackcloth and clothed me with joy,
that my heart may sing to you and not be silent.
O LORD my God,
I will give you thanks forever.

PSALM 30:11–12

You Are Sufficient

When all that my eyes seem to see
Is the dark and the sadness in me
Deep in my heart I still know
That in everything I feel
Your strength serves to show
That You are sufficient for me
And You are the vision that I need in my eyes

When all I have come to count on slips away
My security's gone
Just as my lips start to pray
Emotions run so deep
That my heart can only say
That You are sufficient for me
And You are the vision that I need in my eyes

WORDS AND MUSIC BY JENNIFER ROTHSCHILD © 1990 ROTHSCHILD MUSIC (ASCAP)

Nine

FOLLOW *the* LEADER

ne of the frustrations Phil and I experienced early
in our married life was our inability to enjoy
recreational activities together.

Phil loved sports! In fact, his claim to fame was that he
once intercepted one of Doug Flutie's passes. I bet you didn't
know I'd married such a jock! Oh, you know who Doug
Flutie is! (Humor me.) He's been a popular pro quarterback.
It's just that when Phil reminisces, he forgets to mention the
fact that he caught the pass in 1977 during a Midget Might
football game. Suffice it to say that the man is crazy about
sports and wanted to find one we could enjoy together.

But what? Tennis? No, you both have to be able to see
the ball. Golf? Maybe, but it's slow and expensive.

Canoeing? Ouch! Just the thought of it makes my wimpy arms ache. Jogging? Why? To run round and round in a vicious circle just to work up a sweat? I don't think so!

I guess it's becoming apparent that my lack of involvement in sports has little to do with my blindness. It has more to do with the fact that if I'm going to engage in something slow and expensive that makes me tired and sweaty, it's most likely to be shopping. Now that's healthy!

But Phil was determined, and one day he came home with something he was sure would remedy our (actually, his) frustration—a bicycle built for two. At first, I thought it was a great idea. I knew that I'd be on the backseat and that I could pretend to pedal and let him do all the work.

But then...I began to have second thoughts. Seated aft, I wouldn't be piloting the ship, and knowing that I would have no control on our maiden voyage made me feel a little uneasy. Even so, off we went!

TRAVELING IN TANDEM

I gripped my handlebars—and even began to pedal! It was a typical southern Florida late afternoon, breezy and warm. But as we rode down the intercoastal waterway in West Palm Beach, it was as hard for me to enjoy the trip as it was for Phil to hide his excitement. My uneasiness had given way to quiet panic.

My life is in his hands! I thought. *I don't have any control here!* Then it dawned on me: *I have to tell Phil how to maneuver this bike, or I'm a goner!* So I immediately began to bark commands from the backseat.

"Slow down!"

"I hear an in-line skater; veer left!"

"Move right. You're too close to the seawall!"

I went on and on! Oh yes, he could see perfectly; and oh yes, I was blind. But the woman in me knew my role: My job was to micromanage.

Suddenly, the bike came to an abrupt stop.

"Honey," a very tense, controlled voice said from the front seat, "Will you *please* stop telling me how to steer the bike?"

I said nothing. I wouldn't dignify that unreasonable request with an answer. How dare he? I know we hadn't been married all that long, but he still should have known that I was just doing my job. He had encroached on my turf, so I wielded the most effective weapon in the female arsenal—silent sulking. If my words couldn't put me in charge, my silence sure could!

Well, I was wrong on both counts, and when the ride ended, my analysis began. (The best part of having a degree in psychology is that I can analyze myself for free and no one else has to know how goofy I really am.) I admitted to myself that Phil was right and vowed that I'd try hard to relax and let him drive.

As we geared up for another ride the next night, I still felt uneasy. I didn't like feeling that I wasn't in control. But I was determined—I was a changed woman! We took the same path as the evening before, but this time I held on to the handlebars a little more loosely and barely pedaled. (I liked that part.) As we glided along, I began to notice the tang of saltwater and feel the moist sea air as it caressed my cheeks. I could smell the blooming gardenias and hear the majestic palm fronds batting in the wind. The sound of children's laughter and squeaky tricycles serenaded us.

I was pretty sure those gardenias hadn't bloomed overnight. They had been just as fragrant yesterday. The music of tricycles and palm fronds had been just as melodic the night before. I simply hadn't noticed. On my first night on the backseat of a bicycle built for two, I had been so consumed with being in control that I'd missed the essence of the journey.

"Are you okay back there?" Phil asked after a while. "You're so quiet."

"Oh yes," I sighed. This wasn't silent sulking; this was wordless wonder.

Still, riding on the back of the bike is always just a little unsettling. After all, it's a place where we aren't in charge, and even when we trust the driver, we can still battle feelings of wanting to be in control. Following the one on the front seat is even more difficult when our journey takes us through thorny places that make us feel particularly weak or helpless.

The apostle Paul had some kind of affliction that made

him feel that way. In 2 Corinthians 12:7 he tells us that "there was given me a thorn in my flesh, a messenger of Satan, to torment me." Then he goes on to show us how to chart a course through thorns.

CHARTING A COURSE THROUGH THORNS

Scholars who have studied Paul's life have speculated that his thorn could have been a physical ailment like epilepsy or failing eyesight. Or perhaps it was his persecutors. Or maybe it was that he was single and lonely and longed for the companionship of a spouse.

We can't know for sure. I believe that the Bible doesn't tell us what it was because that information isn't necessary for us to understand what God wants us to know about thorns and how to manage them.

A thorn is anything that makes us feel that we are not in control of our lives. Paul had a thorn, I have a thorn, and you have a thorn. Thorns are a part of the fallen world in which we live. Unfortunately, we often don't deal with them very effectively. Here are a few examples of how we sometimes mismanage the weaknesses in our lives. Do any of these ladies look familiar?

First, there's the "matchless martyr." This helpless heroine wears her thorn as a badge of Christian martyrdom. She displays her thorn proudly for the benefit of all those "who have *no* idea what true suffering really is." She uses her thorn to create feelings of guilt and punish those whose lives are way too easy. She lifts up her thorn to God as her humble sacrifice, reminding Him and everybody else of her elite status in the kingdom.

Then there's the "perfect Pollyanna." This pristine princess disguises the scars her thorn has left. She plasters on a smile and hides her suffering behind a facade of religious rhetoric. Regardless of the pain her thorn might be causing, instead of crying, she emits a series of bouncy platitudes like "Praise the Lord" and "Isn't God good?"

And let's not forget the "determined denier." This militant mama has the lumpiest rug in town because she's constantly shoving her thorn under it—as if disowning it will make it go away. She's not into blaming or sugarcoating; she's into denying.

Of course, these are caricatures. But we can see ourselves and others in them because at times we can all go to theatrical lengths to disguise our weaknesses and feel in control.

Paul, however, shows us a better way to deal with our thorns. He didn't deny that he had a thorn, and he didn't pretend that he liked it. "Three times I pleaded with the Lord to take it away from me," he writes (2 Corinthians 12:8). I can understand that. I've felt that way before, and I bet that you have, too. Our thorns cause us pain and suffering, and like Paul, we need to lift them to God in prayer.

But like Paul, we should also be content with however God chooses to answer our prayer. The answer Paul received was the best answer God had to offer—but it

wasn't to remove the thorn. God gave Paul something better. Even though Paul pleaded with God to take it away,
God said to him, "My grace is sufficient for you, for my
power is made perfect in weakness" (v. 9). Paul received the
grace to deal with his weakness so God could show His
strength through it.

A thorn should never be a platform for drawing attention
to ourselves.

- If I used my blindness as a badge of martyrdom, I
  would be glorifying myself.
- If I sugarcoated the suffering associated with my
  sight loss, I would confuse people and distort the
  true message of God's grace. God *is* good, and He is
  worthy of our praise, but it is equally true that
  thorns hurt and it's okay to cry.
- Shoving my thorn under a rug would only trip me
  up. If I denied the frailty associated with my blindness, I would dismiss the strength of God that can
  abound in my weakness.

Only after I have admitted my insufficiency, yielded it to
God, and received His grace do I have something to boast
about. Paul continues:

Therefore I will boast all the more gladly about my
weaknesses, so that Christ's power may rest on me.

That is why, for Christ's sake, I delight in weaknesses,
in insults, in hardships, in persecutions, in difficulties.
For when I am weak, then I am strong. (vv. 9–10)

Sometimes God delivers us *through* the thorns instead of *from* the thorns. Why? So His grace can grow there. So His strength can sustain us there. And so we can learn how to travel in tandem with Him.

ABIDING BY PASSENGER PROTOCOL

Let's jump on the back of my bicycle built for two and see how this works out in practice. On my second night of traveling tandem, I was able to trade in my desire for control for the joy of following—but only because I had learned some passenger protocol.

Let's take a look at what I learned.

Loosen your grip

On the first night I gripped the handles of the bike so tightly that my knuckles turned white. In a frenzied, futile attempt to stay in control, I grabbed what I thought I could be in charge of and held it in a death grip. Don't we all do this from time to time?

I used to do this with our closet. My husband and I shared one, and let's just say that Phil never really understood the concept behind hangers. His side of the closet looked like a group of men had been crammed in there when the Rapture occurred. Just piles of shirts, belts, shoes, and crumpled pants—all left behind!

When I felt that I wasn't in control of my world, I aimed my sights at his closet. I grabbed on to that and nagged, fussed, and micromanaged until I was convinced that here, at least, was something I could control.

I thought that if only all his shirts were hung according to sleeve length and season, all would seem orderly in my world. I assumed that when all his pants were hung neatly in a row, I would breathe a little easier. But let's face it: I wasn't just trying to control his closet—I was trying to control him!

Well, that kind of control is a myth. It would be easier for me to get the toothpaste on my toothbrush back into the tube than it would be to control my husband or his messy closet. My behavior created only the *illusion* of control, and Phil became pretty *disillusioned* with me because of my controlling behavior. In the end, I still felt the insecurity of being out of control, and he felt the shackles of being overly controlled. I've since learned to grip the doorknob a little more loosely when I open the closet door.

Did you know that an unreasonable desire for control is just another form of greed? Jesus has a lot to say about greed. In the Gospel of Luke, He tells us of a rich man who had such abundance that he didn't have enough room to store it, so he tore down his old barns and built new ones—big as a half dozen Wal-Marts. When he was finished, the rich man said, "Soul, you have many goods laid up for many years; take your ease; eat, drink, and be merry" (Luke 12:19, NKJV).

This man fell for the illusion that he was in control of his world and that all was taken care of for years to come. He's called "the rich fool " because, unfortunately, he died that night and wasn't around to enjoy his bounty.

Greed, however, isn't reserved for material things. If we hold *anything* in our lives in a death grip, it's a manifestation of greed. It may make you feel as though you're in control, but it leads to death. A control freak never enjoys life—and people who share closets with control freaks don't enjoy life either! On the bicycle built for two, I was holding those handle bars in a death grip, and my knuckles turned white because it cut off the blood supply to my fingers.

We all need to be reminded not to choke the life out of things that aren't really important. Jesus said, "Do not worry about your life, what you will eat or drink; or about your body, what you will wear. Is not life more important than food, and the body more important than clothes?" (Matthew 6:25).

So hold things loosely and learn to rest.

Rest where you are

Paul's example of how to chart a course through thorns suggests that we rest in our weaknesses. Until we settle into the position where we've been placed by His grace, we'll never see His strength made perfect there. And we'll never experience the joy of the journey as we follow Him.

Yet instead of resting where God has placed us, lots of us resist. We do this by heaping guilt on others who don't seem to have it as bad, or perhaps by subjecting others to a litany of complaints.

Such behavior is a red flag signaling that we're resisting.

But part of learning to follow is flying the white flag of surrender. We surrender to the position in which God has placed us, and we surrender our behavior in that position.

When you stop to think about it, it takes an incredible amount of effort to gripe and micromanage. What an energy drain! Instead of creating burdens for ourselves by our negative behavior, we should unburden ourselves as we submit all to God and simply rest. Jesus said, "My yoke is easy and my burden is light" (Matthew 11:30).

If you feel that the weight of your circumstances is too heavy to bear, maybe it's because the burden is yours, not His.

On one of my travels, I sat next to a young woman on the airplane. It was her first time to fly, and I marveled at how remarkably calm she was. After a little small talk, I finally asked the question that had been on my mind since we met.

"Why aren't you nervous?" I asked. "Most people are scared, or at least uneasy, on their first flight."

Her answer struck me as very profound and a great example of what it really means to rest. "Well, I'm not a pilot," she said. "Even if something happened, I couldn't do anything about it. So I might as well just relax."

We could all learn a lot from that young college student. Many of us go through life resisting our circumstances because we operate under the mistaken notion that we are in charge. I once saw a bumper sticker that said "God is my co-pilot." That sounds spiritual, but it isn't true. The truth is that on our faith journey, God is the Pilot, and we must follow, not co-lead.

We are not in charge of the journey. We are called to restfully follow. Our Pilot is completely trustworthy. There's no need for us to fret, for He is capable of navigating us through all the turbulence of the journey. We can rest in the very situation where He has lovingly placed us. And when we do, we'll find the fabulous freedom of following.

Once I'd learned to rest on the backseat of the bike, riding in tandem was a pleasure. Instead of rigidly positioning myself for a life-threatening emergency, I decided to relax and enjoy the journey from where I was.

Follow the One in front

As a rookie rider on a tandem bike, I had to learn rather quickly that only one of us could be in front. I found that awfully frustrating because I love to be the one in charge.

For years my desire for complete control masqueraded as the socially acceptable trait of perfectionism. I once was a meticulous housekeeper, burning the midnight oil to make sure that even nonessentials like baseboards and blinds were immaculate. Much to the torment of my family and circle of friends, I insisted that everything in my home match perfectly. And when it came to my clothes, the standard was beyond perfection. I was a prototypical, type-A, firstborn perfectionist!

Well, I'm still a firstborn, but I'm recovering from my perfectionism, because it's really hard to be a blind perfectionist. Blindness has crucified the perfectionist in me, one nail at a time. To follow God, we need to die to our own desires, one nail at a time. "I have been crucified with Christ," Paul writes, "and I no longer live, but Christ lives in me. The life I live in the body, I live by faith in the Son of God, who loved me and gave himself for me" (Galatians 2:20). Our desire to be in complete control denies us the power to live a crucified life. God is the One in front, and living by faith means that God leads and we follow.

My problem on the backseat of a tandem bike wasn't my lack of control; it was my unwillingness to yield my desire for control. As we pedal along on our journey of faith, we struggle with the same tension. It's hard to let go of our desire to be in charge, but the life of faith requires us to trust in the Lord with all our heart and lean not on our own understanding (Proverbs 3:5). Learning to let go of control and willingly follow is essential for traveling the path God has chosen for us.

In the spiritual sense, the backseat of a tandem bicycle is a place of submission, where we yield control to the One who is trustworthy, capable, and knows exactly where we need to go. He alone can get us there by the best possible route. How silly it is for us who are shortsighted to bark commands at the One who sees all eternity.

Since God Himself goes before us and prepares the way, following His loving leadership is always the surest and safest way to travel.

"If anyone would come after me,
he must deny himself and take up his cross daily and follow me.
For whoever wants to save his life will lose it,
but whoever loses his life for me will save it."

LUKE 9:23–24

Satisfied

I'm satisfied with Jesus
I'm as happy as can be
I'm satisfied with Jesus
And Jesus is satisfied with me

I've heard it said a time or two
"I can't get no satisfaction"
And when I start to sing the blues
I have that same reaction
But in searching for significance
I've finally found the key
That Jesus is satisfied with the likes of me

I'm satisfied with Jesus
I'm as happy as can be
I'm satisfied with Jesus
And Jesus is satisfied with me

My soul is finally satisfied
For He is all I need
And that is why I testify
My spirit has been freed

Jesus has accepted me
My heart He's rearranged
No matter what the circumstance
My opinion doesn't change

I'm satisfied with Jesus
I'm as happy as can be
I'm satisfied with Jesus
And Jesus is satisfied with me

Ten

LAUGH *at* YOURSELF

~

One afternoon, Joni's daughter came home from school after a long day of testing. Hannah was a first-grader, so this was her first experience with standardized tests.

"Well, Hannah," Joni asked, "how did the tests go?"

Hannah's response was tentative. "Fine," she said. But her face reflected her concern, and she quickly added, "Except that…well…Mom, I think I got an F in sex."

An F in sex? Joni asked herself. *What in the world is she talking about…and what in the world was on that test?*

When Joni questioned Hannah further, Hannah said that after she wrote her name at the top of the test booklet, the teacher came by and marked an *F* under her name next to the word *sex.*

"Honey," Joni said. "The F stands for *female*—not *fail!*
They just wanted to know whether you're a girl or a boy.
You're a girl, so your sex is female."

Hannah heaved a sigh of relief, and they both began to
laugh.

What a perfect illustration of what it's like to be human!
Often operating on incomplete information and with lim-
ited understanding, we do what is required of us, giving it
our best shot. Yet when we're asked for a self-assessment,
most of us cautiously respond, "Fine… I think I'm doing
fine." Then all of a sudden…*wham!* A big F—failure! Even
the smallest failure can take the steam out of our self-
esteem.

So how do we keep our self-esteem intact when it's
threatened by blunders that make us feel small or stupid?
We all should have a plan because all of us will bungle
something in life. Some gaffes are huge; others are small.
But regardless of the size of the mistake, laughing is the wisest response. Archbishop Edward McCarthy once said that
the ability to laugh at ourselves is a sign of maturity in the
faith.

Why is it, then, that many of us find it so hard to laugh
at ourselves? I think there are a couple of reasons. One is
that we tend to take ourselves too seriously. Another is that
we tend to give more weight to others' opinions of us than
we do to what God thinks of us. Both things rob us of the
humility that allows us to laugh when we feel humiliated.

Not long ago I had a makeup mishap that was really pretty funny—even though I sure didn't think so at the time!

The Key to Giggling at Gaffes

If you've ever had a bad hair day, you'll probably agree that we women tend to wear our self-esteem atop our heads. Now, you might assume that one of the fringe benefits of blindness is that you can't tell when your hair looks really bad. Not so! I don't have to see my hair in the mirror to know that it looks ugly—I can feel it!

I had just cut my hair. It had been pretty long and really big. One of my friends from Texas constantly commented that I had Texas hair. Oh, I did. It weighed as much as my first child and had gotten so big over the years that I needed to either get it cut or move to Texas. Well, I wasn't moving, so under the scissors I went! I was told that it looked cute, but I had trouble styling it.

This particular day I was preparing to speak at a local women's event. The hair was done—in fact it was over-done—and I knew it looked bad. Admitting defeat, I laid down my brush in frustration. Then I remembered something: A friend had given me lipliner and eyeliner pencils from the new cosmetic line she was selling. I don't usually wear liners, but under the circumstances I decided to use them. *It might give me a special look*, I thought, *and maybe no one will notice my hair.*

I meticulously applied the lipliner and then the eyeliner. I imagined how attractive I must look and, with bolstered confidence, headed for the door. As I passed through the living room, I spoke to my son, who was playing Nintendo. He obviously looked up at me when I spoke, because he said, "Mom, your lips are black."

"They are not black," I said. "This is raisin lipliner. It's just more dramatic than you're used to."

"Okay," he said, and went back to his video game.

Then I heard the garage door open. Phil had come to take me to my speaking engagement. He was a little late, and I ran to meet him. He came into the house just as I approached the door, and with more panic in his voice than I'd ever heard, he exclaimed, "Jennifer, your eyes are flaming red!"

Well, it was perfectly obvious at that point that I'd mixed up the makeup. Those were some excellent cosmetics. I had to scrub off the top layer of my skin to remove them. (Here's the practical application for the female reader: If you're having a bad hair day, just put lipliner on your eyes and eyeliner on your lips. I guarantee that it will give you a special look and that no one will notice your hair!)

Even though my mistake wasn't serious, I felt like a fool, and no one wants to feel that way. I couldn't laugh at my mistake because I took myself way too seriously.

Let's face it: We're all pretty serious about ourselves. Sure, we can sometimes struggle with a faulty self-image or low self-esteem, but believe it or not, deep down we still love ourselves. We all do! We love ourselves enough to care on some level what other people think about us. Don't panic— that's not an indictment of our spirituality; it's just part of being human. The problem occurs when we overdo it. Do you realize that taking ourselves too seriously is simply pride? *Ouch!* Now that *could* be an indictment of our spirituality!

Pride is our veiled attempt to protect our fragile ego from being exposed and feeling small. Deep down, what we really seek is honor. We want to be honored by others, and we want to know in our heart that we are worthy of honor. But pride never brings us true honor and respect...only humility does.

The Bible tells us that "a man's pride will bring him low, but a humble spirit will obtain honor"(Proverbs 29:23, NASB). Pride cannot laugh at itself. Only humility allows us to respond with a giggle to even the greatest gaffes.

Even though I always want to present a poised representation of who I am, sometimes that's just not possible, because I'm capable of doing some awfully embarrassing things. Proverbs 17:22 tells us that "a cheerful heart is good medicine," and believe me, I've made enough humiliating mistakes to learn that laughter really is the best balm for a bruised ego—even when my mistakes are a lot more embarrassing than just mixing up my makeup.

THE BEST BALM FOR A BRUISED EGO

I was on my way to Jacksonville, Florida, for a speaking engagement, and by the time my plane landed at the Atlanta airport for a short layover, I had a *big* problem.

My bout with kidney stones had occurred several months earlier, and anyone who has survived that torture will understand why I was determined never to let it happen again and why it's eight glasses of water a day for me. When the plane landed at 11:30 A.M., I had already consumed four of the eight and, well...*I had to go!*

No problem, I thought, *when the airport helper arrives, I'll ask her to take me to the ladies' room*. But when the flight attendant placed my hand on the arm of my escort, I knew something was wrong. *This arm can't belong to a female*, I thought. *The only thing fuller than this bicep is my bladder! My escort is a man!*

I decided that I would "hold it" rather than ask Mr. Muscle to take me to the ladies' room. I knew my layover was short, as was the next leg of my flight, so I began to pray for bladder grace. *Bladder grace?* Well, if you've ever needed it, you know exactly what it is. (Praying for bladder grace, however, includes a prayer of repentance for all the years you failed to do Kegel exercises.)

My escort and I arrived at my gate, and he seated me. Seconds after he left, an announcement came over the intercom: My flight was delayed! *Yikes!* My prayer for bladder grace became more fervent. As my sense of urgency intensified, so did my plea. But then it happened: I learned that there's a statute of limitations on bladder grace. I had reached it, and I was a desperate woman.

Because of my sight loss, my other senses are heightened, and as I sat there, I listened intently to what was going on around me. I felt certain that there was a restroom to my left across the thoroughfare. Desperate women do desperate things, and I flicked out my cane and walked gingerly (because of the bladder, not the blindness) toward the place where I heard all the voices trail off, as if they were entering somewhere. Soon I could hear suitcases rolling onto tile and the sound of running water. I was right! Relief was in sight…well, figuratively speaking.

Most airports have the same kind of setup for their facilities—a large opening in the wall with a bathroom to the left for women and one to the right for men. So I veered to the left, made the final turn into the restroom, and breathed a deep sigh of relief.

Then suddenly there was silence. Total, deafening silence.

Please tell me I'm not in the men's room, I prayed.

Make it so, I thought.

"I am not in the men's room!" I announced.

Maybe their left-brained circuitry had overheated from the shock, because at first all I heard in response were male voices stuttering, "Uh…uh…oh…uh…."

Then came the voices of three older women who had

quickly followed me into the bathroom. "Honey, honey," one of them cried, "you're in the men's room."

"Well, help her—she can't get out!" cried the second woman, who was obviously in charge of the rescue mission.

With seamless choreography, one grabbed my right arm, the other fastened herself fiercely to my left arm, and the two of them swept me away. The third lady stayed behind me, mumbling as she juggled the bags. Awkwardly, we shuffled around the corner into the ladies' room, where the Golden Girls led me to a stall. Three geriatric Rockettes and a blind woman hoofing it from the men's room to the ladies' room. We must have been quite a sight!

When I was once again seated at my gate, I felt my face flushed with humiliation. *The ladies at the senior center are going to hear about this for months,* I groaned. I kept thinking, *Oh no, I could be sitting next to the very guys from that men's room!*

But the longer I sat there, the funnier the bathroom incident seemed. I just kept picturing those men standing there like statues in a wax museum of the shocked and terrified. *Which was worse?* I wondered. *A blind woman watching them, or three women their mothers' age giving them the once-over?*

I began to laugh, and by the time I got back on the plane, my bladder wasn't the only thing that felt relieved— my heart did, too! Laughter truly is good medicine!

The Steam in Self-Esteem

When I had to be hustled out of the men's bathroom, my ego was bruised. I was very worried about what people would think of me and so embarrassed that I wanted to hide.

But guess what? In situations like that, God *wants* me to hide. He wants us all to hide—in Him! "You are my hiding place," says the psalmist. "You will protect me from trouble and surround me with songs of deliverance" (Psalm 32:7). When we hide in God, we realize that our sense of self is derived from His opinion of us, and that delivers us from fear of the opinions of others.

God takes each of us so seriously that He knows the number of hairs on our heads. He knew all the days we would live before they ever were. He knew that there would be bad hair days and days like the one in the men's room. He knew the times when we would look very silly and feel awfully stupid. But no matter how many embarrassing mistakes we make, God's opinion of us never changes. That's why our self-worth should never be based on how others perceive us or on what we see in the mirror. Instead, it should be based on the way *God* perceives us and on what we see in the mirror of His Word. True self-esteem comes from God's esteem, so when you feel humiliated, remember what God says about you:

- You will never be rejected. (1 Samuel 12:22)
- You are His very own. (Isaiah 43:1)

- You are honored and precious. (Isaiah 43:4)
- You are loved with an everlasting love. (Jeremiah 31:3)
- You are accepted by the Beloved. (Romans 15:7)
- You are purchased at great price. (1 Corinthians 6:20)
- You are a new creation in Christ. (2 Corinthians 5:17)
- You were chosen to be blameless in His sight. (Ephesians 1:4)
- You are His workmanship created for a great purpose. (Ephesians 2:10)
- You are defined by His righteousness. (Philippians 3:9)
- You are royal and holy. (1 Peter 2:9)

Do you see how serious God is about you? David was astounded by that realization:

When I consider your heavens, the work of your fingers, the moon and the stars, which you have set in place, what is man that you are mindful of him, the son of man that you care for him? You made him a little lower than the heavenly beings and crowned him with glory and honor. (Psalm 8:3–5)

Can you even fathom the truth that the God of the universe clothed Himself in humanity just to come find you because He loved you and you were lost? I believe that truly understanding how much God loves us and how committed He is to us will evoke true humility.

We may still struggle with feelings of inadequacy and embarrassment, but what we struggle with isn't the same thing as who we are! Part of the gift of being human is wrestling with the wrapping paper. Just because we sometimes feel inept when we blunder doesn't mean that we *are* inept! It means we're *human*. True self-esteem rests on who we are in Christ, and remembering what God thinks of us allows us to respond to our human failings with humility instead of humiliation.

Humility is the key to a healthy self-image because God is the One who puts the steam in our self-esteem. James reminds us that when we humble ourselves before God, He lifts us up (James 4:10). Realizing that God takes us so seriously that He hides us in Himself frees us from taking ourselves too seriously and from fearing what others may think of us.

And then we can laugh.

She is clothed with strength and dignity;
she can laugh at the days to come.

PROVERBS 31:25

Find You Here

Here I am again
Back in the place I always run to
And I know that I will always find You here
I know that You will wipe away each tear

I know that in this place
I will always find Your grace
When I pray I know
I will always find You here

Captured by the moment of my prayer
Drawn by Your mercy to a place of gentle care
And I know that I will always find You here
I know that You will wipe away each tear

I know that in this place
I will always find Your grace
When I pray I know
I will always find You here

Words and music by Jennifer Rothschild © 1990 Rothschild Music (ASCAP)

Eleven

CRY WHEN *You* HURT

ne dark, dreary January afternoon I received a disheartening phone call. It was from Lori. When I heard her somber, frail voice, I immediately asked, "Did he die?"

Our beloved friend Thierry was valiantly fighting a losing battle with cancer, and we knew that a miracle was the only remaining hope for healing this side of heaven. Our hearts were heavy with sadness over his suffering, and they were breaking for his wife, Diane, and their three small kids.

"Not yet," Lori whispered, "But Hospice tells us that it will be sometime today."

Lori had faithfully attended to Thierry and Diane for many months, so I specifically asked, "How are you, my friend?"

Finally she said, "I can't cry."

"Why not?" I asked.

"I don't know how to cry and still remain strong and hopeful, " she said.

Wow! I've felt that way before, and I bet you have, too. Lori echoed the sentiments a lot of us feel when our hope lies on a deathbed.

Over the years as I've struggled to learn how to handle all the emotions that accompany blindness—feelings of frustration, anger, loss, and sadness—God has tenderly taught me how to cry to Him, how to release my sorrow, and how to be strengthened by those very tears.

I think that I had to learn to cry because I misunderstood the purpose of tears. For a long time I mistakenly assumed that the weight of tears would undermine my strength. You've heard the phrase "reduced to tears." It makes it sound as though crying is the final, most debasing result of sorrow, as if our tears weaken us and make us smaller.

But that's not true.

Releasing our sorrow to God doesn't lead to weakness; it generates supernatural strength. Crying never washes away hope into an ocean of despair; it helps cleanse the eyes of our souls so we can more clearly see the source of our hope.

I'm learning that allowing myself to feel the weight of painful emotions—allowing myself to cry out to God even if I don't shed tears—enables me to roll the burden of those emotions onto Him. But before I could learn to cry, God had to open my spiritual tear ducts.

WHEN TEAR DUCTS ARE BLOCKED

When I was an infant, the doctors discovered that I was unable to cry. Oh, I went through the motions, but no tears ever came because my tear ducts were closed. The doctors had to surgically open them in order for me to cry.

As it turned out, I needed the same thing spiritually.

For years after I became blind, my immaturity and pride kept me from the healthy response of crying. I needed God to lay His healing hand upon me and open my spiritual tear ducts.

One day when I was in my early twenties, Darlene, my next-door neighbor and one of my best friends, came for one of her frequent visits. I had just finished vacuuming, and as Darlene settled onto the couch for a chat, I wound up the vacuum cleaner cord and turned to put the vacuum in the closet. As I swung it toward the closet, I did a full body slam into the open door.

"*Ouch!*" Darlene yelled.

I remained unusually silent.

"What? What?" she asked. "Are you okay? Why don't you say something?"

With bridled control, I calmly responded, "If I don't *act* like it hurts, it won't hurt so much."

Years later, I recall that painful moment and just shake

my head. *What was I thinking?* I had obviously overdosed on pop psychology. It's just plain silly to think that not acknowledging an injury will somehow ease the feeling of pain. Sometimes life hurts! And when it does, we can admit our pain and cry.

Now, let me be clear. When I speak of learning to cry, I don't necessarily mean only the physical act of shedding tears. I mean allowing ourselves to have an honest, heartfelt response of sorrow or grief when it is warranted. Some of us cry over Folgers coffee commercials, and some of us don't cry even at funerals. Crying is as individual as each personality. But in order to really experience life, we need to abandon our pride and reservations and humbly admit our sorrow, our pain, and our needs. All of us need God's touch on our spiritual tear ducts. To be tenderly in touch with our own humanity allows us to cry, and when we do, we feel the strengthening hand of our Great Physician.

Thierry went to heaven on January 16, 2002. At his funeral two days later, my friend Lori cried. She released her sorrow to God as she cried tears of sorrow mixed with tears of joy. And I have a feeling that as she cried, Jesus wept, too.

WHEN JESUS WEPT

"Jesus wept."

I take great solace in this, the shortest verse in the Bible (John 11:35). These two words, if correctly understood, can help us learn to cry.

The Gospel of John tells the story of Jesus' beloved friend Lazarus of Bethany. When Jesus was teaching beyond the Jordan, Lazarus fell gravely ill. His sisters, Mary and Martha, sent word to Jesus, but the Lord stayed where He was for two more days before setting out for Bethany. By the time He arrived, Lazarus had already been in the tomb for four days.

Martha greeted Jesus first. Consumed by grief, she said, "Lord, if you had been here, my brother would not have died" (John 11:21). When Mary's turn came, the Jews who had come to console the sisters followed her from the house. As they approached Jesus, they were all weeping, and Mary echoed her sister's words, "Lord, if you had been here, my brother would not have died" (John 11:32).

John tells us what happened next:

When Jesus saw her weeping, and the Jews who had come along with her also weeping, he was deeply moved in spirit and troubled. "Where have you laid him?" he asked.

"Come and see, Lord," they replied.

Jesus wept. (John 11:33–35)

What a startling passage! Jesus not only allowed man's sorrow to enter Him, but He entered so deeply into man's sorrow that He outwardly expressed His deep emotion. What an amazing God!

You and I are no different from Mary and Martha. We all grieve. But Jesus understands our sorrow. Beyond that, He is *moved* by our sadness and grief. So trust Him with your tears. They are precious to God. "You keep track of all my sorrows. You have collected all my tears in your bottle. You have recorded each one in your book" (Psalm 56:8, NLT).

The Bible tells us that Jesus wept on one other occasion. He had just come down from the Mount of Olives, and "as he approached Jerusalem and saw the city, he wept over it" (Luke 19:41). Jesus' gaze extended far beyond Jerusalem's beautiful temple, busy marketplace, and bustling crowds. He saw into the future. He saw what would eventually become of the city. He knew that within decades Jerusalem would lie in ruins—its beloved temple demolished, its commerce destroyed, its citizens dead or scattered to the wind. He saw the needless, self-inflicted suffering of those who rebel against God's will—and He wept.

I think that the same is true today. I believe that when God looks into our hearts and sees the pain we have inflicted on ourselves by resisting Him and His gracious will, He weeps. God's tears always flow from a heart of compassion. "The LORD is good to everyone. He showers compassion on all his creation" (Psalm 145:9, NLT). Our God longs to protect us from unnecessary suffering. He longs to comfort wounded souls, heal broken hearts, and lovingly lead us. His tears are those of a brokenhearted and compassionate friend.

It would be difficult to trust our tears to One who never cried. But "we do not have a high priest who is unable to sympathize with our weaknesses" (Hebrews 4:15). Knowing that Jesus wept can minister deeply to us. But has it ever occurred to you that our tears can also minister to Jesus?

WHEN WE CRY

Let's join Jesus at a dinner in the courtyard of the home of a rich Pharisee named Simon. Back then, the houses of wealthy folks were often built around a courtyard in the shape of a hollow square, and when a rabbi came to dine, all sorts of people would come to learn from him. That would explain why a certain woman was at Simon's house that day. Luke calls her an "immoral woman" (Luke 7:37, NLT), which means that she most likely was a prostitute.

Jesus was reclining at the table, and when the woman approached Him, she was overcome and began to weep. Round her neck she wore a little bottle. It was called an alabaster, and she wanted to honor Jesus by anointing Him with the perfume in it. As she stood behind Him weeping, her tears fell upon His feet, and so she lovingly began to kiss them, pour the perfume on them, and wipe them with her hair.

That's a beautiful picture of abandoned love. For a Jewish woman to loose her hair in public was very immodest. Now I know that it might seem that a prostitute could easily disregard such a provincial view. But she was in the home of a religious man and in the presence of Jesus. I think that the picture we see of her loosening her hair to wipe His feet shows that she had forgotten about everything but Jesus. Mary of Bethany, who was not an "immoral woman," also anointed Jesus with oil and wiped His feet with her hair (see Matthew 26:6; Mark 14:3; and John 12:3). For both women, it was as if nothing and no one else really mattered at that moment.

What makes this scene so striking is the contrast between Simon and the prostitute. Although it was customary for the host to wash the feet of a guest, to give him the kiss of peace, and to anoint his head with a drop of attar of roses, Simon had done none of those things, as Jesus reminded him:

"Do you see this woman? I came into your house. You did not give me any water for my feet, but she wet my feet with her tears and wiped them with her hair. You did not give me a kiss, but this woman, from the time I entered, has not stopped kissing my feet. You did not put oil on my head, but she has poured perfume on my feet. Therefore, I tell you, her many sins have been forgiven—for she loved much. But he who has been forgiven little loves little."

Then Jesus said to her, "Your sins are forgiven." (Luke 7:44–48)

I think that if we look in the mirror, we'll find ourselves looking a lot like either Simon or that woman. Which of them really experienced the presence of Christ?

Some of us, like Simon, are religious, good, and moral. We invite Jesus in and are enlightened by His teachings, but we remain unmoved by His presence. We spread before Him all our achievements and wealth, much like Simon spread the meal before Jesus. Simon was pretty impressed with himself. He thought he looked good in the eyes of man and God, and since he was conscious of no need in his life, he felt little love for Jesus. Jesus came to Simon's house, but Simon totally missed out on His visit.

While Simon's self-sufficiency kept him from really knowing the One with whom he dined, the woman was overwhelmed with her need...and it opened the door to the forgiveness and love of God. That's why she cried. Her tears of gratitude were the outward sign that inwardly she had totally abandoned herself to Him. The woman came to Simon's house, and she left intimately connected to Jesus.

Don't ever think that your tears of repentance, gratitude, and love don't touch the heart of God. He is blessed and ministered to when you abandon yourself to Him. The religion of Simon did not minister to Jesus; the woman's love did. Don't allow your religion to be a shallow substitute for really knowing and experiencing the presence of Jesus in your life. Instead, cry out to Him. Your tears will not only be a sweet offering of worship, they will also promote the health of your soul.

WHEN THE SOUL CRIES

We often see tears as just the outward manifestation of an inward emotion such as sorrow, pain, anger, or even joy. But actually, tears promote the health of the human eye. In the same way, soul-tears—crying out to God—make an extraordinary contribution to the health of our souls. When you realize that God has a spiritual as well as physical purpose for the tears you cry, you'll understand why not one of them is shed in vain.

Tears cleanse

Physical tears wash unwelcome debris off the surface of the cornea of the eye. If you've ever been at the beach on a windy day, you know how true that is! Just one tiny grain of sand in your eye can cause the tears to gush. God has created a wonderful device to cleanse your eyes.

He has also created an amazing mechanism to cleanse your soul. It's what I call shedding soul-tears—allowing yourself to cry out to God in prayer from the bottom of your heart. Throughout the Psalms we hear the sound of David's soul-tears as he cries to God in prayer. "Give ear to my words, O LORD, consider my sighing," he writes. "Listen to my cry for help, my King and my God, for to you I pray" (Psalm 5:1–2). When David was rejected, slandered, pursued, and threatened on all sides, he chose to cry out to God in prayer. "Wicked and deceitful men have opened their mouths against me; they have spoken against me with lying tongues. With words of hatred they surround me; they attack me without cause. In return for my friendship they accuse me, but I am a man of prayer" (Psalm 109:2–4).

Sometimes the winds of life blow hard. Harsh words, rejection, and cruelty can rip a hole in our heart, and the debris they create can threaten to lodge there. That's why we need to cry—to allow soul-tears to flow from our heart to God's. David says that the Lord "is near to all who call on him" and that "he hears their cry and saves them" (Psalm 145:18–19). That doesn't necessarily mean that God removes the hard situation. But crying out to Him invites Him to begin to deliver us *through* the heartache by washing away the devastating debris so it can't lodge in our being.

Tears protect

Recently, Connor and I were attempting to display our patriotism by planting small flags along the front yard line. I showed him how to gently twist the wooden dowel as he pushed it into the grass. But we had no sooner finished planting the first pole than he quickly jerked it out of the ground. Well, I was still bent over him, so the jagged end of the flagpole jammed into my open eye.

Wham!

It was definitely a patriotic moment—I saw stars and stripes forever!

My eye began to flood in response to the dirt-covered invader. I had a scratched cornea, and for several days my eye seemed to produce enough tears to cause dehydration. But the doctor told me this was the best thing for my injury, because physical tears have an antibacterial effect on the eye that helps protect it from infection.

When our soul cries tears to God, we can be assured of the same kind of protection. Crying out invites the Great Physician to protect us from greater infection. If we cry tears of bitterness to God over a broken heart, that bitterness cannot become more deeply rooted or spread. When we cry tears of guilt to God over regrettable choices, that guilt cannot grow into depression and anxiety. To allow ourselves to cry to God the tears that only our soul can produce will bring healing as we release everything to Him.

WHEN WE COME AS WE ARE

One of the most poignant lessons I learned about crying happened in a Florida women's prison. A Bible teacher asked me to come to her class one Saturday afternoon to provide music for the inmates who attended the study. I was a little anxious to begin with, but after I was thoroughly frisked and my keyboard was almost completely disassembled, I was really nervous! What would these women be like? I had no idea what to expect.

After I set up my keyboard, the guard ushered in about twenty women. They were very quiet. There was no introduction. The Bible teacher just told me to "go ahead and start." I was so far out of my element that I started just as I would have at a church setting where everyone was eagerly responsive. Well, that went over about as well as an opera singer at a hoedown! I very quickly sensed that I needed to change my approach. So I took a giant leap outside my comfort zone and blurted out, "What would you like to sing?"

Silence.

Then a gruff voice called out, "Just As I Am"!

"You mean the old hymn?" I asked. I was a little surprised because it seemed to me that it wasn't a song that even most churchwomen enjoyed. It was one of those hymns they endured at the end of the service while they gathered their Bibles and purses and made covert plans for lunch.

The Bible teacher jumped in. "Jennifer, this is Sandy. She's been here for several years...."

"For manslaughter." Sandy finished the sentence.

"Yes," the teacher continued, "and since she came to Christ, 'Just As I Am' has been her favorite song."

Feeling very moved, I played the introduction, and as we began to sing, the weeping also began. Sandy was so overcome with emotion that she couldn't voice the words, and the Bible teacher pulled out a tissue and began to wipe away her own tears.

I've never heard "Just As I Am" sung more sweetly. On that day I understood Charlotte Elliott's words "Just as I am, without one plea" in a way I never had before. These women knew what it was to plead before a judge and jury. They understood what it meant to be declared guilty. I realized how little I really knew and understood about my own guilt and pardon. I also had trouble singing the words that day because I, too, wept. Just like Sandy, I was guilty— "without one plea, but that His blood was shed for me."

When we truly know how much we are forgiven, and when we embrace how much we are loved, we will learn to cry. Someday "there will be no more death or mourning or crying or pain" (Revelation 21:4). On the day we are released from our earthly shackles and stand before our Lord, He will lovingly cup each of our faces in His gentle hands and wipe every tear from every face once and for all. Until that day, our tears allow us to feel His healing touch every time we cry to Him.

The righteous cry, and the LORD hears
and delivers them out of all their troubles.
The LORD is near to the brokenhearted
and saves those who are crushed in spirit.

PSALM 34:17–18, NASB

Someday

Someday I'm gonna leave it all behind me
Someday I'm gonna fly where no pain will find me
I'm leaving all the suffering,
I'm leaving all the heartache
They won't confine me someday

Tears they fall so hard
They wound my tender soul
Taking me off guard
As if I'd never known
That someday this will be
Just a faded memory
And my eyes will finally see

Childishly I look at life
And scornfully I cry
Shaking of my fist
And wanting to know why
But someday I will be
In the place prepared for me
And my eyes will finally see

Someday I'm gonna leave it all behind me
Someday I'm gonna fly where no pain will find me
I'm leaving all the suffering,
I'm leaving all the heartache
They won't confine me someday

When I go I'll leave this world behind me
And then I'll know
I'll be free from all that binds me

Someday I'm gonna leave it all behind me
Someday I'm gonna fly where no pain will find me
I'm leaving all the suffering,
I'm leaving all the heartache
They won't confine me someday

WORDS AND MUSIC BY JENNIFER ROTHSCHILD AND CRAIG ALEA

© 1993 ROTHSCHILD MUSIC (ASCAP)

Twelve

Wait *on* God

When Phil and I had been married about a year, he was the director of student life at Palm Beach Atlantic College. Part of his job was to oversee the student body's formal banquets, so twice a year I had to squeeze some money from our tight budget to buy a formal dress. This time it was homecoming, and I was prepared! I'd just found a beautiful black dress at a bargain price.

The morning of the banquet, I got everything together. Shoes, earrings, hose...*yikes!* I only had white hose! I needed *black* hose! I called Phil at work to let him know about our latest family emergency. He was busy moving tables, dealing with caterers, and coordinating the student decorators, so to say that he wasn't available right then would be an under-statement.

I realized that I'd have to wait. Now, it probably doesn't seem like a big deal at this point. After all, it was still morning. But on hectic days like this one, Phil often changed into his suit at the hotel. So I knew there was a good chance that I might not get my black hose in time for the six o'clock dinner, and I was already anxious.

By 5:45 P.M., I was fully dressed. My makeup was meticulously applied and my hair was done. I was a picture of well-groomed perfection—from the knees up, that is! I still had no black hose. All my waiting had been to no avail, and now I was really worried.

At this point any guy reading this is probably screaming, "Wear the white hose, lady! Wear the white hose!" Male logic is often ludicrous to a woman. I would go without hose before I'd risk being arrested by the fashion police for committing such a crime against good taste. No, I would wait it out.

Well, between moving tables and flower arrangements, Phil had evidently communicated my crisis to my friend Darlene, and at 5:56 she burst through my door.

"Black hose!" she proudly announced. I pulled the coveted hose from the package. Within seconds I had them on my grateful legs and, after a long day of waiting, I was on my way to the banquet.

Because of my sight loss, I've had to learn to wait. The

day of the homecoming banquet, I spent the entire afternoon wondering how I was going to get black hose and wishing I could just jump in the car and go buy it. But I can't drive. So when it comes to even the everyday needs of life, I've had to master the art of delayed gratification. I have to wait until someone else is heading to the store. I get my needs and desires met according to someone else's schedule, rarely my own.

I've learned that although waiting is never fun, it's always healthy. It's like spiritual weightlifting: It strengthens us by teaching us that our joy and peace and hope don't depend on when our needs and wants are met. Instead, they come from what we choose to do in the meantime, when life is hard and so is waiting.

The Way We Wait

We all have to learn to wait for some things in life, and the way I see it, there are three ways of waiting and three kinds of waiters—and I don't mean the kind at a banquet! I bet you'll recognize yourself in one of them.

First, there's the *worried waiter.* If you took a snapshot of her, you'd see her wringing her hands and pacing the floor. She's so busy calling her friends to bemoan her circumstances that she forgets to take them to God in prayer. Then there's the *wishful waiter.* She never lives in the present moment because her energy is tied to "what if," not to "what is." She spends most of her time speculating on what it will be like when the wait is over, and until then she just aimlessly tries to get through each day. Finally, there's the *wise waiter*. She's focused on God's face, not on His hand—not on what He will do for her, how He will take care of her situation, or when He will end her wait. She is waiting only on God, and she is present, peaceful, and productive.

What kind of waiter are you? Are you present where you are, or do you pine away over things that are not? Are you wringing your hands, or bending your knees? Are you waiting on God alone, or waiting for the wait to end?

Many of us spend our lives "in the meantime," waiting for something we want or need: a better job, a less stressful time in life, a newer car. We endure the wait, and then, the prize—a promotion, a long vacation, a zero-percent car loan—only to have a new need, a new wait, and a new prize pop up in its place.

Sometimes the wait is much more difficult because the prize seems much greater.

For some of us, the prize is healing.

For others, deliverance from suffering.

For many, the lifting of a heavy financial burden.

The prize is often the thing that keeps us faithful while we wait. But what if all our joy isn't reserved for the award ceremony? What if there is something deep and precious in the in-between time? If our focus is on the prize alone, we can't help but see the waiting as a trial, and when we do, we can miss the joy of the journey and overlook the treasures along the way. Learning to wait for the small things or the big things in life is healthy because it teaches us that our joy doesn't depend on whether we have them or not. It teaches us to experience the strengthening effect of "in all" joy, not just "end-all" joy.

So what do we do while we wait? How do we make the meantime meaningful?

We can find great meaning during the waiting times of our lives by delighting in God. Psalm 37:4 says, "Delight yourself in the LORD and he will give you the desires of your heart."

I believe that's true when we delight in anyone. When I delight in my husband, I am mindful of and interested in his desires. In fact, they often become my desires. If I'm not delighting in him, there's no way I want to spend three long hours sipping coffee at one of those megabookstores, surrounded by books I can't even read. And besides, I don't even like coffee! But if I am delighting in him, I want to be there and sip right along with him.

Sometimes we look at Psalm 37:4 as a blank check. We think that if we delight in God, He will give us what we want. But the emphasis of the verse is on *delighting*. When we delight in God, He places in us the desires He wants us to have. "It is God who works in you," Paul reminds us, "to will and to act according to his good purpose" (Philippians 2:13). When our delight is in God, our desires will be what

He wants for us instead of what we want for ourselves.

God desires peace and contentment for all of His children, and I have found that the more I delight in Him, the more that becomes the desire of my own heart. Oh yes, healing would be an extraordinary prize—a treasure—and God may give it to me someday. But I would still ultimately lose if I were physically whole but lacking spiritually. Without peace and contentment, the joy of healing would be fleeting and shallow, but resting contentedly in Him reveals a depth of grace that I can still be reveling in ten million years from now in His presence, in His house.

Worry prevents us from experiencing peace and contentment. So if you happen to be a worried waiter, forget about calling up your friends to bemoan your situation. Here's the only phone number you need to remember: 1-800-CALL-GOD.

Jeremiah, the weeping prophet, knew God's number by heart: "Then you will call upon Me and come and pray to Me, and I will listen to you" (Jeremiah 29:12, NASB). Through the ages, God has urged all those who are worried and troubled to phone home. "Call upon Me in the day of trouble; I shall rescue you, and you will honor Me" (Psalm 50:15, NASB).

God's prescription for the worried waiter is "Do not be anxious about anything, but in everything, by prayer and petition, with thanksgiving, present your requests to God" (Philippians 4:6). If you do, "the peace of God, which transcends all understanding, will guard your hearts and your minds in Christ Jesus" (v. 7).

I am convinced that my deep desire for peace and contentment is a direct reflection of the heart of the God in whom I delight—a treasure He wants to give me in the meantime, while I wait.

Think about your own desires. What are they? If you could fulfill the desire of your heart, what would it be? The answer to that question will reveal where your delight truly lies.

Align your heart with the heart of God, and your desires will reflect His.

WAITING AND HOPING

I am not often overly emotional about my blindness. My usual approach is to face it with resolve. But one night was different. It was almost as if I'd been given permission to feel the loss more deeply, to wish that things were different, and to question why God had not healed me. It was like peeling back a Band-Aid very slowly from a tender wound, still sensitive to the touch.

That night I was returning home from singing at a prayer conference led by Dr. Waylon Moore. I was deeply moved in my spirit by what had transpired. Lori had gone with me, and on the way home we began to discuss why God had not healed me. Was it His will? Was it sin that had held back His hand of healing? Was it a lack of faith? Was it okay not to be healed? Didn't that reflect poorly on God? The ride home ended long before we exhausted the possibilities, so we sat in the driveway for another hour.

Feelings like these aren't easily plumbed or expressed, much less resolved, and at last we decided to explore them further when our bodies and spirits weren't so weary. I asked Lori to read me Psalm 63 before she walked me into the house, and by the dim light of the driveway she began to read: "My soul waits in silence for God only...."

"Oh," she said, "that's Psalm 62, not 63!"

"Read it again," I said, "that's the best mistake you ever made."

Lori continued to read. "My soul, wait in silence for God only, for my hope is from Him. He only is my rock and my salvation, my stronghold; I shall not be shaken" (Psalm 62:5–6, NASB).

On that night of painful questioning, those verses became the words that my spirit could not articulate alone. I felt as though I really had looked into the face of my Healer and come so close to Him that I'd heard Him speak to me. He told me that my hope for healing is in Him alone. Therefore, my soul can wait—wait as long as it takes, even if it never happens here on earth. He alone—not my healing—is my rock and my refuge. My deliverance from blindness is not my source of hope...He is.

When we pin our hopes on the fulfillment of our desires, we fall into the trap of wishful waiting. James has some advice for wishful waiters: "You do not know what will happen tomorrow. For what is your life? It is even a vapor that appears for a little time and then vanishes away. Instead you ought to say, 'If the Lord wills, we shall live and do this or that'" (James 4:14–15, NKJV). We can't know if our desires will be fulfilled or not.

Even if we could, we set ourselves up for disappointment when our focus is on the prize instead of on God.

The psalmist had learned where to place his hope. "Lord, where do I put my hope? *My only hope is in you*" (Psalm 39:7, NLT, emphasis added).

When our hope is in God alone, He becomes our prize. That's what Paul meant when he wrote, "I press on toward the goal to win the prize for which God has called me heavenward in Christ Jesus" (Philippians 3:14). Paul's desire was God's desire, his prize was Christ's will for him, and his hope was in God. Such hope will not disappoint us. "In you our fathers put their trust; they trusted and you delivered them" (Psalm 22:4).

If you're a wishful waiter, learn to trust the One who purposefully leads you through long desert stretches on your way to the Promised Land. Don't waste time daydreaming about how tasty the milk and honey will be. Enjoy the manna! God designed it just for you. Be willing to submit your longings to God and wait patiently on Him. Place your hope in the God in whom you delight and you will never be disappointed.

WORTH THE WAIT

Clayton has always been an intuitive thinker and a sensitive child. From the time he was capable of expressing abstract thought, he would say that he wished "Mommy could see." It was important to the little guy. Of course he wanted that for his mom. What child wouldn't?

So I wasn't surprised that one day when he was six, he said, "Mommy, I wish you could see." By then I had grown accustomed to such comments.

"Why do you wish that?" I asked.

"So you could play Nintendo with me," he said, "cause Daddy is really bad at it!"

At the time, Clayton's reasoning made me chuckle. But a year later he became a Christian, and one of the first evidences of his newfound faith was that, unprompted by his dad or me, he began to pray for my healing.

Then one spring day when he was in the third grade, we were playing a game together. I sat on the carpet and waited while he meticulously placed the pieces of the game on the game board. In most of the games we play, I roll the dice and he reads it; I ask him to move the pieces and he moves them. This game, however, was very tactile, and we thought it might be easier for me. He read my rolled dice, and I attempted to move my piece. But no matter how I tried, I just couldn't do it. I was frustrated and Clay was disappointed.

"Son," I said, "you need to choose a different game. This

one just isn't working." Without a word, he began to put the pieces back in the box. He was so pensive that I could almost hear the wheels turning in his mind. When he spoke at last, his comment was very different from the one that had made me chuckle two years earlier.

"Mom," he said, "I was thinking. I don't think God will heal you here on earth."

"Why not, son?" I asked. "Why don't you think God will heal me on earth?"

Clayton's answer has been my greatest lesson on learning to wait. *"If God healed you here on earth,"* he said, *"you might love earth more, and heaven is best."* The seeds of spiritual truth had already been sown in his young heart, and now they were springing up before me with the promise of fragrant blossoms of hope. A wise waiter can wait for what she knows is best—heaven!

I can't help but think of the Negro spirituals, growing out of the shameful practice of slavery in the early days of our nation. So often, these songs are focused on heaven. Life in bondage, life in the cotton fields from dawn till dusk didn't provide much material for songwriting. But heaven? What a richness awaited just over the horizon! What comfort and rest and beauty and freedom—and the Lord Jesus Himself, waiting with open arms! Lacking earthly treasure, their songs focused on the place where true treasures awaited... and that's where their hearts were, too.

When our eyes are fixed on temporal things, like illness,

financial strain, or difficult relationships, it's easy to get discouraged, because most of the time our burdens feel heavy and there seems to be no end in sight. When we keep our attention fixed on earthly things, we can easily lose heart.

But Paul says:

We do not lose heart. Though outwardly we are wasting away, yet inwardly we are being renewed day by day. For our light and momentary troubles are achieving for us an eternal glory that far outweighs them all. So we fix our eyes not on what is seen, but on what is unseen. For what is seen is temporary, but what is unseen is eternal. (2 Corinthians 4:16–18)

Like the psalmist, a wise waiter knows where to fix her gaze: "One thing I ask of the LORD, this is what I seek: that I may dwell in the house of the LORD all the days of my life, to gaze upon the beauty of the LORD" (Psalm 27:4). This is what allows her to redeem every moment of the wait and experience the joy of the journey.

Learning to wait for what is best from God is not the same as learning to wait for healing. To know Him and to allow our suffering to reveal His life in us is far better than the temporal prize of physical healing. Having that kind of perspective in even the most difficult places in our lives allows us to see them as temporary burdens that are fashioning for us a far greater—and eternal—weight of glory. It's as if somehow the suffering of today is immediately invested in a heavenly account that pays eternal dividends, even while we wait. When we fix our eyes on things that are unseen and view hardship through the lens of eternity, we can see that even the terminal is temporal.

Have you ever thought about "the end"?

You know, your funeral, the day your spirit celebrates its homecoming and your body is put to rest in the ground? Of course you have—we all have! One thing I know for sure is that when I die, I want to be buried facing east.

Now facing east might seem like a strange and minor detail to you, but I recently learned from my mother's genealogical research that most of my ancestors have been buried with their graves facing that direction. The reason, she discovered, was that they were sure that when Jesus returned and appeared in the eastern sky, the dead in Christ would rise first (1 Thessalonians 4:16), and they wanted to be positioned in such a way that their first glimpse with resurrected eyes would be the face of Jesus.

Wow! What a testimony—even in death.

That got me to thinking how much more meaningful it would be to *live* facing east. How sad it would be if His glorious appearing found us stuck in the meantime, wringing our hands and stressing out over the small things in life, or missing the joy of the moment by wishing for something other than God's best. We know that the sky can be rolled back at any second, so how much wiser it would be to live in such a way that everything we think and do positions us for His coming.

What a way to wait!

> *Those who wait on the LORD will find new strength.*
> *They will fly high on wings like eagles.*
> *They will run and not grow weary.*
> *They will walk and not faint.*

ISAIAH 40:31, NLT

When Faith Becomes Sight

It's been more than twenty years now since I left the eye hospital knowing that I would be totally blind. But even on that day, I believed that just beyond my despair a doorway of promise was about to be opened by the merciful hand of God. It was the promise that *no matter what my circumstances, it could be well with my soul.* That's why even amid deep sorrow, I could go home, sit down at our old piano, and play "It Is Well."

God knows about great sorrow. He is a Father who watched His only Son suffer and die. When His beloved Son Jesus cried, "It is finished," the Father's heart must have been rent in half, just like the temple veil.

"It is finished" was so final, so certain.

Yet for us that cosmic closure became a gateway of hope.

On a hill called Calvary, God Himself made a way for us to have soul-wellness. When Jesus was suspended between heaven and earth on the cross, He made a way for it to be well with our souls once and for all. If we choose to receive His gracious offering of love, which He demonstrated through His death on the cross, His grace makes it well. Unfortunately, some of us close our eyes to the goodness of God and turn a deaf ear to His beckoning voice.

Joni Eareckson Tada was paralyzed in a diving accident when she was a young woman. Since then she has been confined to a wheelchair, and it has been there that God has taught her the greatest lessons about Himself. In her book *Diamonds in the Dust*, Joni recounts being asked if, given the choice, she would choose life in a wheelchair. Listen to her response:

I can't think of anyone who desires to be paralyzed. Who would be foolish enough to choose not to have the use of his legs and hands? Can you imagine someone wanting to be blind? Choosing darkness over the brilliance of a clear blue sky? And who would want to be deaf? Who in the world would desire silence instead of the beauty of a waltz or the soothing voice of a loved one? Yet there are people who choose to be handicapped.... Theirs are very serious disabilities, not physical ones but spiritual handicaps.[2]

Jesus Himself spoke of those with self-inflicted handicaps when He said, "You will be ever hearing but never understanding; you will be ever seeing but never perceiving. For this people's heart has become calloused; they hardly hear with their ears, and they have closed their eyes. Otherwise they might see with their eyes, hear with their ears, understand with their hearts and turn, and I would heal them" (Matthew 13:14–15).

The greatest handicap you can have is for it not to be well with your soul. To allow your circumstances to blind you to the infinite goodness of God is far more debilitating than physical darkness. To silence the voice of God who longs to tell you of His love and forgiveness is far worse than physical deafness. To be paralyzed by fear is far more confining than physical immobility.

We all have handicaps—flaws and weaknesses that remind us that we are clothed in humanity. Yet living with human handicaps is not nearly as difficult as living with the devastating consequences of a calloused heart. We can never experience what it really means to live if we harden our heart toward God and refuse to allow Him to make it well with our souls.

If I had to make the choice, would I really choose soul-wellness over physical sight? Having wrestled with that question in the deepest part of my longing, I can honestly answer that I would. Why? Because I've learned that I can function, even thrive, without sight, but I'm convinced that

I cannot live without soul-wellness. I know that I would barely function—and certainly not thrive. If blindness is the one illuminating force in my life that can reveal the depth of wellness I can possess, then I gratefully welcome it.

I'm convinced that to have soul-wellness, to have found the life I've dreamt of, has been worth the cost. To find such a life is worth *any* cost. God doesn't demand our suffering as an exchange for this blessing. Oh no, He is kind and merciful. Yet in His mercy, He sometimes allows us to suffer so we can shake off the things that crowd our thoughts, weigh heavy on our hearts, and keep us from Him. But giving ourselves completely to Him in utter abandon and faith allows us to receive life—life that cannot be shrouded by darkness, silenced by deafness, or stilled by paralysis.

I don't know what it's like anymore to look into people's faces. It's been many years since I saw a face clearly. I know that as a child I looked into my mother's face, with its soft olive skin, and I know that I looked into the sweetness of my dad's dancing blue eyes and watched his forehead wrinkle when he was in deep thought. I looked into the freckled faces of my sometimes annoying, but always adorable, brothers, and I looked into the wise eyes of my beloved grandparents.

What fascinates me is that even though I know I saw all those precious faces, in my memory they are now draped in shadows, blurred and indistinguishable. It's a strange phenomenon. Even so, it excites me—because unless God chooses to heal me here on earth, the very first face I'll see with clarity will be the face of Jesus. Awesome thought!

I'll always remember how Mike, my mobility instructor, wrapped up my first lesson of learning to walk in the dark. After he had walked me all around my neighborhood, he called my attention to some blooming hibiscus on the corner near my home.

"When you smell the flowers," he said, "you know you're almost home."

Always remember that for each of us there will come a day when we too will smell the flowers and know we're almost home. The closer we get, any kind of darkness here on earth—the depth of suffering it may represent, the difficulties that it may make us recall—will pale in comparison to the sweet aroma that will usher us into the presence of the One whose face we will clearly see. And when our eyes look into His face, we'll realize that, compared to the surpassing excellence of seeing Him, nothing else really mattered.

That's when our faith becomes sight.

And Lord, haste the day when my faith shall be sight
The clouds be rolled back as a scroll
The trump shall resound, and the Lord shall descend
Even so, it is well with my soul

Let's Keep in Touch

Thank you for allowing me to share part of my journey with you through the pages of this book. I would love to hear about your journey as well, and I invite you to visit me at JenniferRothschild.com, where we can keep in touch through my e-mail newsletter. On my Web site you can also find information about my music albums that contain the lyrics you have just read, along with a Bible study companion to this book.

Meanwhile, my prayer for you is that "the eyes of your heart may be enlightened in order that you may know the hope to which he has called you, the riches of his glorious inheritance in the saints, and his incomparably great power for us who believe" (Ephesians 1:18–19).

God speed you on your way as you learn to walk by faith, not by sight.

Jennifer

Jennifer Rothschild
4319 South National, Suite 303
Springfield, MO 65810
www.jenniferrothschild.com

Notes

1. Derek Redmond story adapted from *Experiencing God: The Musical* by Gary Rhodes and Claire Cloninger (Nashville, Tenn.: Genovox Music Group, May 2000).
2. Joni Eareckson Tada, *Diamonds in the Dust* (Grand Rapids, Mich.: Zondervan, 1993), devotional for February 15.

Experience God's Touch

RECOGNIZING GOD'S TOUCH ON YOUR LIFE

JENNIFER ROTHSCHILD

Formerly Touched by His Unseen Hand

1-59052-530-2

To a blind person, human touch is essential. In the absence of facial expressions, it reassures and comforts. But can you still feel the warm and soothing touch of an unseen God? Author and musician Jennifer Rothschild, who lost her vision at the age of fifteen, explains how God's touch works from the inside out, warming the heart, mind, and soul. It lifts weights that eyes could never see. It washes away the anguish of guilt, the bite of fear, and the ache of loneliness. With the gentle pressure of His hand on our shoulders, we can find our way through the darkest of nights.

Thy word is a lamp unto my feet,
And a light unto my path.
PSALM 119: 105 KJV

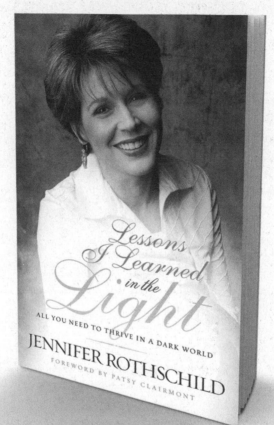

Have you known darkness? Are you there even now? There is a ray of hope that brings clarity and guidance: God's Word—the Light that is better than life. No matter what you face today, *Lessons I Learned in the Light* will help you cling to His Word, be God-conscious, drop the baggage and enjoy the fishbowl.

Available in bookstores and from online retailers

Other Great Resources by Jennifer Rothschild

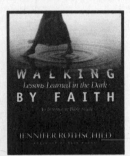

Walking by Faith
Bible Study Member Book

Based on *Lessons I Learned in the Dark*, this workbook features six weeks of interactive material for daily personal study. Includes leader guide.

ISBN 0-6330-9932-5

Walking by Faith
Bible Study Leader Kit

Includes one member book with leader guide and two DVDs that contain seven teaching segments, music videos, and bonus footage.

ISBN 0-6330-9145-6

Walking by Faith
The Music Captured Live

Experience the seven songs you heard during the bible study, plus three additional songs, including a reprise of the traditional hymn, "It is Well with My Soul."

UPC 8-09812-00502-5
Music CD

Walking by Faith
The Music Videos

Enjoy the beauty and gracefulness of the music videos from the *Walking by Faith Bible Study*. Includes family life bonus footage and interviews. On DVD.

UPC 8-09812-00509-4
DVD Video

Along the Way
Songs from the Early Years

You can hear the most requested songs from two of Jennifer's earlier albums, "Out of the Darkness" and "Come to the Morning." If you enjoyed the music from *Walking by Faith*, you'll treasure the music and lyrics Jennifer wrote "along the way."

UPC 8-09812-00492-9
Music CD

find these and other products at
WWW.JENNIFERROTHSCHILD.COM

Keep in touch with Jennifer
Jennifer Rothschild • 4319 S National, Suite 303, Springfield, MO 65810
ph: 417.888.2067 • email: JR@jenniferrothschild.com

Almond Roca

1 cup Butter
1 cup Brn sugar
   melt in sauce pan
line cookie sheet w/ salt
pour sugar over

400° 5 min
sprinkle w Cho. Chips
   in oven 1 min. more
smooth out chocolate
& sprinkle w/ chopped
nuts & put in freezer

   Thurs. 29th 10:00 & lunch

"privledged planet" movie